KEY
WOMEN
WRITERS
EDITOR SUE ROE

ELIZABETH
BARRETT
BROWNING

KEY
WOMEN
WRITERS
EDITOR: SUE ROE

ELIZABETH BARRETT BROWNING

ANGELA LEIGHTON

Indiana University Press
Bloomington

Manufactured in Great Britain

Library of Congress Cataloging-in-Publication Data

Leighton, Angela, 1954–
    Elizabeth Barrett Browning.

    (Key women writers).
    Bibliography: p.

    1. Browning, Elizabeth Barrett, 1806–1861—Criticism
and interpretation.   I. Title.   II. Series.
PR4194.L45   1986   821'.8   85-45957
ISBN 0-253-30101-7
ISBN 0-253-25451-5 (pbk.)

1 2 3 4 5 90 89 88 87 86

For H.

Titles in the Key Women Writers Series

Key Women Writers
Series Editor: Sue Roe

The *Key Women Writers* series has developed in a spirit of challenge, exploration and interrogation. Looking again at the work of women writers with established places in the mainstream of the literary tradition, the series asks, in what ways can such writers be regarded as feminist? Does their status as canonical writers ignore the notion that there are ways of writing and thinking which are specific to women? Or is it the case that such writers have integrated within their writing a feminist perspective which so subtly maintains its place that these are writers who have, hitherto, been largely misread?

In answering these questions, each volume in the series is attentive to aspects of composition such as style and voice, as well as to the ideas and issues to emerge out of women's writing practice. For while recent developments in literary and feminist theory have played a significant part in the creation of the series, feminist theory represents no specific methodology, but rather an opportunity to broaden our range of responses to the issues of history, pyschology and gender which have always engaged women writers. A new and creative dynamics between a woman critic and her female subject has been made possible by recent developments in feminist theory, and the series seeks to reflect the important critical insights which have emerged out of this new, essentially feminist, style of engagement.

It is not always the case that literary theory can be directly transposed from its sources in other disciplines to the practice of reading writing by women. The series investigates the possibility that a distinction may need to be made between feminist politics and the literary criticism of women's writing which has not, up to now, been sufficiently emphasized. Feminist reading, as well as feminist writing, still needs to be constantly interpreted and re-interpreted. The complexity and range of choices implicit in this procedure are represented throughout the series. As works of criticism, all the volumes in the series represent wide-ranging and creative styles of discourse, seeking at all times to express the particular resonances and perspectives of individual women writers.

Sue Roe

Contents

Acknowledgements

My thanks, first of all, to recent editors and critics of Elizabeth Barrett Browning, on whose scholarship I have depended and to whose interpretations I have often been indebted—particularly Cora Kaplan, Dorothy Mermin and Dolores Rosenblum. Secondly, my thanks to all the friends and colleagues who have been so generous with their time in reading and commenting on various chapters, especially James Booth, Harriet Marland and Marion Shaw, but also Rachel Hawes, Tom McAlindon, Patsy Stoneman and Rowland Wymer. I am grateful, as well, to Margaret Elliott, my expert and patient typist. Lastly, my thanks to successive generations of students in the 'Women in Literature' course at Hull, who have contributed their interest and ideas to the shaping of this book.

Abbreviations

Boyd

Elizabeth Barrett to Mr. Boyd: Unpublished Letters of Elizabeth Barrett Browning to Hugh Stuart Boyd, ed. Barbara P. McCarthy (London, John Murray, 1955).

Diary

The Barretts at Hope End: The Early Diary of Elizabeth Barrett Browning, ed. Elizabeth Berridge (London, John Murray, 1974).

'Glimpses into My Own Life'

'Glimpses into My Own Life and Literary Character (1820)' in 'Two Autobiographical Essays by Elizabeth Barrett', *Browning Institute Studies*, 2 (1974), 119–34.

Horne

Letters of Elizabeth Barrett Browning Addressed to Richard Hengist Horne, 2 vols, ed. R.S.T. Mayer (London, 1876–77).

Kenyon

The Letters of Elizabeth Barret Browning, 2 vols, ed. Frederic G. Kenyon (London, 1897).

Letters: 1845–1846

The Letters of Robert Browning and Elizabeth Barrett 1845–1846, 2 vols, ed,

Elvan Kintner (Cambridge, Mass.,
Harvard University Press, 1969).

MRM   *The Letters of Elizabeth Barrett Browning to*
               Mary Russell Mitford: 1860–1854, 3
               vols, ed. Meredith B. Raymond and
               Mary Rose Sullivan (The Browning
               Institute and Wellesley College,
               1983).

Ogilvy   *Elizabeth Barrett Browning's Letters to*
               Mrs. David Ogilvy: 1849–1861, ed.
               Peter N. Heydon and Philip Kelley
               (London, John Murray, 1974).

References to *Aurora Leigh* are by volume and line
number only, and are from *Aurora Leigh and Other Poems*,
introduced by Cora Kaplan (London, The Women's
Press, 1978). All other published poems are from *The*
Complete Works of Elizabeth Barrett Browning, 6 vols, ed.
Charlotte Porter and Helen A. Clarke (New York,
Thomas Y. Crowell, 1900).

Elizabeth Barrett Browning:
Brief Chronology

1806	Birth, 6 March
1820	*The Battle of Marathon*, privately printed
1826	*An Essay on Mind, with Other Poems*
1828	Death of Edward Barrett (Bro)
1833	*Prometheus Bound . . . and Miscellaneous Poems*
1838	*The Seraphim and Other Poems*
1840	Death of brother Edward (Bro)
1842	'The Book of the Poets' written for the *Athenaeum*
1843	*A New Spirit of the Age* written collaboratively with R.H. Horne
1844	*Poems* (2 vols)
1845	Correspondence with Robert Browning begins
1846	Marriage to Robert Browning and journey to Italy
1849	Birth of Robert Wiedemann Barrett Browning (Pen)
1850	*Poems* (2 vols), revision of 1844 edition including *Sonnets from the Portuguese*
1851	*Casa Guidi Windows*
1856	*Aurora Leigh*
1857	Death of Mr Barrett
1860	*Poems Before Congress*
1861	Death in Florence

Chapter One

Elizabeth Barrett Browning: Woman and Poet

In April 1850, a notice appeared in the *Athenaeum* which proposed a candidate for the newly vacated post of Poet Laureate. The writer, who was probably H.F. Chorley, listed three reasons why the appointment of a woman might be appropriate: it would be 'an honourable testimonial to the individual, a fitting recognition of the remarkable place which the women of England have taken in the literature of the day, and a graceful compliment to the Sovereign herself.' His appreciation of the female literary spirit of the age does not in itself, however, justify the appointment of a woman. He adds, scrupulously, that 'there is no living poet of either sex who can prefer a higher claim than Mrs. Elizabeth Barrett Browning.'[1] At this time neither the *Sonnets from the Portuguese* nor *Aurora Leigh* were known to the public. It was Barrett Browning's 1844 collection of poems which was considered of sufficient merit to gain her this high and reputable standing as a poet. In the event, however, the successor to Wordsworth was named as Alfred Tennyson.

1

By 1932, when Virginia Woolf published an essay on *Aurora Leigh* in *The Common Reader*, Barrett Browning's reputation had suffered a surprising and severe decline. Woolf praises *Aurora Leigh* warmly as 'a masterpiece in embryo',[2] but her assessment of its author's fame in the early 1930s is a melancholy one. She laments that 'fate has not been kind to Mrs. Browning as a writer. Nobody reads her, nobody discusses her, nobody troubles to put her in her place.'[3] The reasons for this fall into obscurity are hard to specify. One may have been the general Modernist reaction against the eminent Victorians in the 1920s and 1930s. Another may have been an intellectual reaction against that seamy and sentimental interest in Barrett Browning's life, which started with the publication of her letters at the end of the nineteenth century and was encouraged by such popularising biographical works as Rudolph Besier's play, *The Barretts of Wimpole Street*, in the early decades of the twentieth century. One other reason may have been the steep rise in Robert Browning's reputation at this time, against which his wife's was often disparagingly measured. But whatever the precise reason, it is true that Barrett Browning's fame as a poet declined steadily in the early twentieth century, and sank into obscurity, in England, for nearly fifty years after Woolf's attempt to revive it. Only with the growth of feminist publishing and criticism in the late 1970s has this tide been turned, and her poetry come to be read again, discussed and put in its place. That its place is much higher than a century of neglect suggests, is one of the rewards of this concerted act of recuperation.

The rise and fall of Barret Browning's reputation makes a dramatic graph of changing critical fashions and tastes. In her own lifetime, her poetry very often received high acclaim. The reviews of her first mature collection of 1844 were prestigious and encouraging. The publication of the *Sonnets from the Portuguese* in 1850 and of *Aurora Leigh* in 1856 provoked rapturous acclamations, particularly from other writers and poets. The *Sonnets* were eagerly and favourably compared with the sonnet sequences of Petrarch and Shakespeare, for instance, and *Aurora Leigh* with the epics of Homer and Milton. On the announcement of her death in 1861, there was a flood of reappraisals of her work. These were often unstintingly enthusiastic. She was hailed, for instance, as 'the greatest poetess the world has ever known' and as 'the Shakespeare among her sex'. She was ranked 'among the chief English poets of this century', and even, as one critic was prepared to testify, 'with Homer, Dante, Shakespeare, Milton, Goethe, and Shelley'.[4] Her being pre-eminent among her own sex was no bar, at this time, to joining the company of the greatest male poets.

However, at the beginning of the twentieth century it is possible to detect two distinct changes of attitude in the critics. First, there is a new preoccupation with stylistic smoothness and correctness. 'She is one of the most irregular of writers',[5] Hugh Walker complained in 1910. Other critics deplored in particular her fondness for wayward colloquial metres and for half rhyme.[6] Osbert Burdett in 1928 echoed a widespread opinion when he praised exclusively 'the beautiful strictness of her sonnets'.[7] This change in taste, and its accompanying obsession with technical correctness, resulted in a depreciation of the very strengths of Barrett Browning's poetry. G.K. Chesterton's is a rare voice at this time to applaud her 'hot wit', her 'high-coloured' language and 'love of quaint and sustained similes'.[8]

Secondly, however, and even more damagingly, there was a new preoccupation with the criterion of womanliness among the critics. The publication of Barrett Browning's letters, at the end of the nineteenth century gave impetus and encouragement to a personalised, biographical and sexually partisan literary criticism. In 1897, Kenyon's edition of her letters, which contained many biographical notes, answered an already increasing interest in her life; while in 1899, the publication of the love letters of 1845–1846 amply gratified the avidly sentimental curiosity of both critics and public. These letters in particular helped to fuel the new, heady, chivalrous admiration for the woman, which then characterises much critical writing at the turn of the century. An idealised image of the woman gradually supplants the figure of the poet in the critics' imagination, and Elizabeth Barrett Browning comes to be known, not so much as one of 'the chief English poets of this century', but as the heroine of a love story. One sign of this new romanticising strain is that *Aurora Leigh* tends to be dismissed as a hectic aberration, while praise is lavished on the *Sonnets from the Portuguese*. Behind this change in literary tastes there is evidently also an ideological bias which has more to do with woman's appointed role than with the merits of poems. To love is a more womanly calling than to write.

The result of this romantic idealisation is that the woman and the poet become separate and irreconcilable figures. Furthermore, admiration for the one very often entails an implicit depreciation of the other. This prejudice in favour of the woman at the expense of the poet is ingenuously expressed by Oliver Elton at the end of his book on *The Brownings* (1924). Although this is offered as a study of both poets, Elton devotes only the last thirteen pages to Elizabeth, and these are largely a personal eulogy of the woman. 'Altogether,' he concludes, 'we leave Mrs. Browning with a mixture of admiration and discomfort. Her faults of form and phrase are never the faults of smallness; it would have been an honour to have known her. Often we feel we would rather have known her than read her'.[9] Not only does the image of the woman contend for Elton's attention against the poems themselves; that image also provides a form of compensation for the technical shortcomings of those poems. Barrett Browning's 'faults of form and phrase' are quickly excused and dismissed in the thought that 'it would have been an honour to have known her.' Elton's confessed predilection for the woman finally provides a reason for not reading her poetry at all: 'we would rather have known her than read her'.

It is clear that the image of the woman here is being balanced in an opposite sliding-scale of values. The woman weighs against the poet, the wife against the artist, and Elton's preferences for the first subtly confirm a negative literary judgement. The extent to which this is not just a harmless quirk of taste is revealed by the frequency with which the attribution of womanliness is used, at this time, as a way of damning with loud praise. The more exalted the woman, the more excusable her errors of versification. Osbert Burdett shows the true aim of such negative flattery when he announces, simply, that the 'verse of Elizabeth was too womanly to be the verse of a great poet.'[10] The idea that womanliness is a virtue in competition with greatness is the unadmitted and enduring basis of the chivalrous imagination.

Just how intoxicating the legend of the woman had become is revealed by Lilian Whiting's book, *A Study of Elizabeth Barrett Browning* (1899). In spite of its title, this is an extravagant hagiography, which extols the woman's virtues and ignores the poet's works. 'The life of EBB,'

Whiting claims, 'is a more potent influence for enlight-enment and uplifting in the world to-day than it was even when her visible presence was on earth. It was expedient for us that Jesus should go away.'[11] This infatuated biography perpetuates an image of the woman as saint rather than poet. Whiting frames her author in stained glass and describes her life as a swift spirit's progress: 'from the time we see Mrs. Browning as a child with the golden light of the oriel window falling on her brown curls touching them with gleams of gold, until she fades from our sight . . . we see her as a spirit passing.'[12] To such airy legends as these the decline of Barrett Browning's reputation as a poet must be partly attributed.

But there is another side to this worship of the woman which is not so harmlessly devout. Eric S. Robertson opens his book, *English Poetesses* (1883), with the testy pronouncement that 'Ladies who write verse now-a-days do not care to be called "Poetesses"; yet, as they have not had the wit to find a better designation for themselves, the name must serve.'[13] The book goes on to lay bare its prejudices with a rich mixture of sentiment-ality and malice. It is Robertson's confirmed opinion that 'Women have always been inferior to men as writers of poetry; and they always will be',[14] and he proves the point by appeals to their womanly nature. 'What woman,' he asks magniloquently, 'would not have been Niobe rather than the artist who carved the Niobe?' and answers, with the confidence of his own soaring rhetoric: 'More than poetry, and more than man, woman loves the children who fall from the heavens, like the pure snow, to hide earth's blackness.'[15] This spectacu-larly inexact biological explanation for the artistic inferiority of women carries a strong moral fiat as well. Just as Southey's famous injunction to Charlotte Brontë that 'Literature cannot be the business of a woman's life' slides into the moral compulsion that 'it ought not to be',[16] so Robertson's assertion, that women love children first of all, carries the moral tag that it is their duty to do so in order to help 'hide earth's blackness'. The fact that Niobe's fate was to see her seven sons and seven daughters killed, and to weep for them eternally, betrays the strongly punishing streak in Robertson's sentimentality.

It is this widespread, pious iconography of womanhood which sadly corrupts many critical assessments of Barrett Browning's work at the turn of the twentieth century. Even Besier's play, *The Barretts of Wimpole Street* (1931), which brings to the story of her life a new Freudian slant, ultimately does little more than perpetuate the legend of the good woman. Besier hints at Mr Barrett's repressed incestuous love for Elizabeth, and the idea finds striking visual support in the fact of the poet's helpless invalidism. Confined to her bed for much of the play, she is the invitingly passive and seductive object of its sexual theories. For Besier, the figure of the woman still takes precedence over the figure of the poet, and the story of her love for Robert over the other story of her lifelong commitment to writing. This last flurry of popularity in the 1930s thus only culminates a long period of merely sentimental and intrigued interest in the facts of Barrett Browning's life.

But after the 1930s, interest in both her life and verse fails, and the name of Barrett Browning receives only brief and honorary mention in works of criticism. From this half-century of neglect recent feminist critics have rescued her, and have proposed that her poetry be read and discussed again. To free Barrett Browning's name from the web of pious legend and sweet romance that has entangled it for so long must be the first task of any

7

new critical evaluation. Only then will the strong, idiosyncratic and crusading voice of this woman poet be heard in its own right.

Barret Browning's own comments about women and women's rights are not always sympathetic. She admits to her friend and literary confidant, Miss Mitford, for instance: 'I am *not*, as you are perhaps aware, a very strong partizan on the Rights-of-Woman-side of the argument . . . I believe that . . . there IS an *inequality* of intellect' (*MRM*, III, 81), and to Robert she confides the same belief that 'there *is* a natural inferiority of mind in women—of the intellect . . not by any means, of the moral nature' (*Letters: 1845–1846*, I, 113). In *Aurora Leigh* she strongly condemns those who 'prate of woman's rights,/Of woman's mission, woman's function' (VIII, 819–20),[17] not because she disbelieves in those rights, but because she thinks the cause will be furthered by work rather than by theories. The principle of equality between the sexes is to be found in the principle of equal work. As Aurora tells Romney near the end:

> The honest, earnest man must stand and work,
> The woman also—otherwise she drops
> At once below the dignity of man,
> Accepting serfdom.
>
> (VIII, 712–15)

The whole argument of the poem is that Aurora proves her right to work against Romney's offer of 'serfdom' in marriage. Furthermore she proves herself, whether we believe it or not, more able to influence society by writing than he by philanthropic works. She thus defines her poetry as a political instrument of change. Barrett Browning's 'feminist' purpose is rooted, not so much in her actual social message, as in her commitment to *write*, as a woman, against the odds of tradition and of continuing male prejudice.

Before J.S. Mill in *The Subjection of Women* called for an end to 'the morality of chivalry' and for a new 'morality of justice'[18] in the social relations between the sexes, women writers were demanding intellectual impartiality from their critics. ' "To you I am neither man nor woman—I come before you as an author only" ', Charlotte Brontë insisted in a letter to her publisher, and Barrett Browning made similar objections about literary discrimination when she wrote: 'I do not at all think that because a woman is a woman, she is on that account to be spared the ordinary risks of the arena in literature . . . Logical chivalry would be still more radically debasing to us than any other' (*Kenyon*, I, 227). It was not only outrage and disapproval which women risked incurring from the literary establishment, but also, and worse, the dishonest flattery of being made a special case. In order to avoid these dangers, many writers in what Elaine Showalter has termed the 'Feminine phase'[20] of women's writing, from 1840 to 1880, attempted to conceal their sex by adopting a male pseudonym. Barrett Browning, however, published all her volumes of poetry from 1844 onwards under her own name, and furthermore often made a point of speaking in them with a self-consciously female voice. As Cora Kaplan notes in her excellent introduction to *Aurora Leigh*, 'Barrett Browning makes the condition of the poem's very existence the fact that its protagonist is a woman and a poet.'[21] Writing, for her, is not a neutral activity, though she too demands an impartial judgement of it. Rather, it is an activity always marked by the vulnerability, ambition and difference of being a woman.

This crusading and self-conscious emphasis on the female voice is the badge of Barrett Browning's literary sexual politics. Clearly she was aware of the prevailing climate of discrimination against which she dared to take up her pen and write. In one letter she urgently confides to Miss Mitford: 'but *you*, who are a woman & man in one, will judge if it is'nt [sic] a hard & difficult process for a woman to get forgiven for her strength by her grace. You who have accomplished this, know it is hard—& every woman of letters knows it is hard. Sometimes there is too much strength in proportion to the grace—and then . . O miserable woman!' (*MRM*, III, 38). It is in this knowledge that she writes the story of the graceless Aurora, who chooses the loveless occupation of earning her living by the pen. The first critics' dislike of the character of Aurora and their objection to female authorship being the subject of an epic poem[22] are indications of how challenging the work sets out to be. By portraying a woman who rejects love in order to write, Barrett Browning seems to be condoning the forfeiture of womanliness to genius, of 'grace' to 'strength'. 'I have a stout pen, and, till its last blot, it will write, perhaps, with its "usual insolence" ' (*Kenyon*, II, 423), she declared a year before she died. That ' "insolence" ' is the mark of her best poetry. By speaking confidently and undisguisedly as a woman, she rudely infringes the subtle codes of sexual decorum which hampered women writers at this time. The 'strength' of her poetic voice very often out-proportions its 'grace', and the discrepancy is made over to the woman's cause.

It is not only Barrett Browning's commitment to write *as* a woman which shows the political bravery of her stance, but also her commitment to write *poetry*. Although, as H.F. Chorley noted in the *Athenaeum*, this was indeed an age of women's literature, it was not an age of women's poetry. G.H. Lewes opened his important review of women's writing, 'The Lady

Novelists' (1852), with the portentous statement: 'The appearance of Woman in the field of literature is a significant fact.'[23] But although novelists might have been grateful for this recognition, the cause of lady poets remained largely unsupported. This absence of a company of kindred women poets is one that Barrett Browning feels acutely, and it is against this absence that her own heroically female voice must be heard. Although two of her poems generously acknowledge the work of her near contemporaries, Felicia Hemans and Letitia Landon, in general she feels her singular and anomalous status with regret. 'I look everywhere for grandmothers and see none,' she writes. The indisputable failure of any strong tradition of women's poetry impresses on Barrett Browning her isolation. But it also impresses on her the strength of the male literary heritage. 'It is not in the filial spirit I am deficient, I do assure you,' she hurriedly informs her correspondent, 'witness my reverent love of the grandfathers!' (*Kenyon*, I, 231).

Whereas the novelists of the period entered 'the field of literature' in comparatively large numbers, Barrett Browning, as a poet, enters alone. Her work everywhere betrays this sense of sexual difference and isolation. She stands at the end of a long and brilliant tradition of 'grandfathers', and her debt and gratitude must be entirely to them. 'All women who write are pupils of the great male writers,'[24] John Stuart Mill pointed out with characteristic perspicuity, and Barrett Browning, much more than her contemporary sister novelists, felt the strength and oppression of this inheritance.

Yet, it is interesting that she defines her relation to these precursors in terms of 'the filial spirit'. The familial terminology comes naturally to her as she acknowledges her literary influences. It is as if the habit of being a daughter, which was so strong a role in her real life, extends to her role as poet. She admires and reverences her past masters 'in the filial spirit' of dependency and respect. But she also looks to them as a daughter, and thus as one whose line of descent from them is uncertain and insecure. As daughter, she cannot hope to inherit their power as naturally and confidently as a son. Her sense of exclusion and singularity as a woman is poignantly expressed in that unanswered cry 'for grandmothers'.

The familial basis of Barrett Browning's description of herself as a poet subtly echoes the facts of her real parentage. Her mother was physically and temperamentally weak, and died early, while her father was a tyrannically dominant and strong-willed man. For forty years of her life, Elizabeth lived under the shadow and power of her beloved father, and to him she dedicated all her early volumes of poetry. The association between her real and her literary fathers is one which motivates and inspires much of her work, and it is in her relation to both of these—in her doubly impressed sense of daughterhood—that her poetic identity develops.

Yet, there is a conflict in this chosen role. As daughter, her relation to the forces of influence is one of loving subjection. The powerful hierarchy of the Victorian family with its emphases on duty and obedience— emphases taken to an extreme by Mr Barrett—only stressed this subjection more strongly. However, as poet, Barrett Browning desires strength and independence for herself, and thus desires to reject the authority of the father. The struggle between the two roles of daughter and poet, between 'reverent love' and jealous ambition, is worked out at a cost in her poetry, even as it was in her own life.

The most powerful literary influence on Barrett

Browning's work naturally comes from the Romantic poets, and from Wordsworth in particular. It is he whom she reverences as the 'poet-hero of a movement essential to the better being of poetry, as poet-prophet of utterances greater than those who first listened could comprehend, and of influences most vital and expansive',[25] as she somewhat pompously expatiates in the *Athenaeum* in 1842. It is from the Romantic poets that she derives her own inspirational theory of poetry— her belief, as she defines it less awesomely, in 'the pneumatic character of [the poet's] gift'.[26] To Robert she puts the matter simply: 'I quite believe as you do that what is called the "creative process" in works of Art, is just inspiration & no less' (*Letters: 1845–1846*, I, 96). The idea of some external aid in writing that might be figured as a presence to the imagination is one which comes to the Victorian poet rich with traditional usage. Such a presence might be a lovely lady, a high muse or merely a spirit of the place—a tentative haunting to allay the Romantic imagination's fear of emptiness.

However, Barrett Browning's figuring of inspiration often differs from these in being closely associated with the members of her own family. While Wordsworth celebrates a notional presence of nature, a nurturing consciousness or pervading spirit of things, she generally connects such forces with the intimately loved figures of her real family, and above all with the figure of her father. It is he who haunts her poetic consciousness and against whom she wages the longest struggle for self-expression. Barrett Browning, the Victorian daughter of the Romantic poets, but also the dutiful daughter to her own father for forty years of her life, naturally associates the figure of the inspiring muse with the figure who dominated her life, both emotionally and practically, for so long.

Thus, it may be said that her poetics depends on an intimate and highly biographical relation to the figure of power that represents her muse. Because she identifies herself so forcefully as a daughter poet, who is strong in 'the filial spirit', she ties herself in imaginative and emotional dependence to the figure of the father. His authority and power are the source of her creativity. However, in order to gain authority and power for herself, she must in some sense dispossess herself as daughter, and break the natural relation of obedience and reliance which ensures that father's continuing love. Although she acknowledges other types of muse in her poetry: the figures, for example, of her ghostly mother, her dead brother, her poet lover and her fallen 'sister', it is her father above all whose inspiration she courts and whose oppression she feels. The risk and cost of this imaginative dedication become everywhere apparent in her work.

Woman Poet or Muse? Some Theoretical Perspectives

Mary Jacobus has identified two mainstreams of recent feminist criticism: the empirical and the psychoanalytical.[27] Empirical criticism interprets the literary text primarily as a piece of documentary evidence which might illuminate the biographical or sociological context of its writing. Psychoanalytical criticism, on the other hand, refers the text to an essentialist theory of the difference between male and female discourse.

However if, as I suggest, the 'feminist' resonance of Barrett Browning's work is to be found in her poetics, rather than in any sociological documentation or linguistic experimentation, neither an empirical nor a psychoanalytical method will quite serve to interpret her

14

poetry. To search out her social and political views is to find that they are often impractical and idealistic, and might be defined only in the broadest terms as liberal and Christian. Her poetic language, on the other hand, is, in her early poems, derivatively Romantic, and in her later poems often prosaic, colloquial and philosophical, As such, it does not lend itself to the kind of sophisticated linguistic analysis which distinguishes the French post-Lacanian theorists of *écriture féminine*, for instance.

The attraction and the danger of much recent psychoanalytical theory is that it seems to offer a 'scientific' model of sexual difference in writing. Feminist critics have therefore naturally looked to this discipline for guidance in the practice of a literary criticism based on gender. However, it might be said that the very abstract authoritativeness of psychoanalytical models of difference makes them liable to become simply self-generating theories, which cannot be used to prove anything except their own point. Furthermore, the very point which might be valuable to feminist criticism: namely, the relation of women to language, tends to exempt itself, by its very dualistic nature, from use. Woman, in Lacanian psychoanalysis, stands as the opposite of man and therefore as 'Other' to his subjectivity and his discourse. As early as 1949, Simone de Beauvoir warned against the dangers of accepting, in theory, dualisms which are all too true in fact. She writes that 'what peculiarly signalizes the situation of woman is that she . . . finds herself living in a world where men compel her to assume the status of the Other.'[28] This warning might apply to certain aspects of contemporary theory as well. That 'He is the Subject . . . she is the Other'[29] has become a fruitful and sophisticated commonplace of this theory. To develop from it a

15

feminist literary practice, however, as some French feminists have done, is to be willing to remain within the limitations of a myth that strengthens the inequalities of existing political and social facts.

The principle of woman as the 'Other' in the psychoanalytic school of Freud and Lacan is a principle which Lacan himself admits derives from 'courtly love'.[30] Maud Ellmann neatly summarises the premise of both the Lacanian and the courtly love schools when she writes: 'A lover's discourse can only really flourish in the absence of the woman, whatever name one calls that absence . . . Discourse is the process by which woman is erased, blanched out.'[31] For all his deconstructing play, the linguistic terms of Lacan's method are dogmatically bound to a gender-dictated dichotomy of subject and object. His theory of the *name of the father*[32] as that which gives access to the Symbolic order of language and culture is a theory which, for all his disclaimers of any sociological or even sexual reference, remains, as far as any followers or commentators might be concerned, deterministically divided according to gender. In his system, woman stands at the place of the 'Other', which is outside the order of language. 'By her being in the sexual relation radically Other,' he asserts, 'in relation to what can be said of the unconscious, the woman is that which relates to this Other.'[33]

In her feminist defence of Lacan, Jacqueline Rose fixes these variable terms in an opposition which already comes to sound more like sociological description. 'As negative to the man,' she writes, 'woman becomes a total object of fantasy . . . elevated into the place of the Other and made to stand for its truth.'[34] She ends by accepting the dichotomy, and derives from it a theory of sexually determined language. She claims that 'femininity is assigned to a point of origin prior to the mark of symbolic difference and the law'; and adds that the 'privileged relationship of women to that origin gives them access to an archaic form of expressivity outside the circuit of linguistic exchange.'[35] She draws the conclusion from Lacan that the mark of being a woman and 'Other' is to have the resource of some special, 'archaic', non-verbal form of expression. This may provide a defining characteristic of the female psyche or it may be a utopian feminist ideal, but it is not a tool for criticism of a nineteenth-century literary text.

In fact, both Rose and the French feminists might be seen to take more than Lacan himself concedes. They use the psychoanalytic association of woman with the 'Other' to support a theory of essential linguistic difference. This is a theory of woman's language as metaphorically expressive of woman's sexuality. Such language is described as 'totally fluent',[36] for instance, or as 'endless' and avoiding techniques of 'closure'.[37] The very ousting of woman from the place of discourse can thus become a cause for literary rejoicing. 'Estranged from language, women are visionaries,'[38] claims Julia Kristeva; and Luce Irigaray gladly affirms at one point that women *are* 'the unconscious'.[39] From this alternative place, women become thieves of language or else they have some special access to the resonances of silence, madness and obscurity. This separatist theory of women's language valiantly celebrates the very fact which gave de Beauvoir her cause for complaint.

However, there is a risk that the abstract dualisms of psychoanalysis are being used here to support a theory of linguistic difference which has as its basis the very simple fact that most seminal theoretical texts have been written by men. It is this suspicion which is wittily acknowledged by Jacques Derrida in his book after Nietzsche, *Spurs*. In it, he playfully exposes the tradition

17

of courtly love which underlies most theories of gender and writing. He announces at the start that 'it is woman who will be my subject',[40] and then proceeds to define 'woman' as that which stands in opposition to the longstanding phallocentrism of western philosophy. But he does so by resorting to the hoary commonplaces of courtship and seduction. He writes that 'woman seduces from a distance. In fact, distance is the very element of her power. Yet one must beware to keep one's own distance from her beguiling song of enchantment.'[41] Derrida merely plays a variation on an old myth, in which 'woman' is the enchanting, unattainable, distant Other. She is the haughty and unruly muse of the man's serious work. She is an inspiration and a nuisance. Thus, he tells, the philosopher writes, and the woman spoils his page and breaks up his truth. But although it is she who gives value to the man's writing, making it different from itself, the fact remains that she has no pen, stylus, spur, phallus or even umbrella[42] of her own. She is defined only in mysterious opposition to everything that distinguishes the male subject who writes: Nietzsche, Derrida, or just 'one'.

In her fine article 'Is There a Woman in This Text?' Mary Jacobus speculates on the role of 'woman' in theoretical works by men, and suggests that the real 'function of the female "victim" . . . is to provide the mute sacrifice on which theory itself may be founded.'[43] Certainly the opposition of man and woman, subject and Other, in many theoretical texts is an opposition between the man who speaks or writes and the woman who is mute. But to accept this muteness as a defining characteristic of women's writing, as some critics have done, is then in a sense to accept the chivalric compensations of the theorist, who gives to the figure of the 'Other' a special status only to strengthen or, it may be, only to deconstruct, his own writing. To develop a theory of women's writing from this theoretical rendering of woman 'as Other' is, as Elizabeth Berg writes, to risk perpetuating her 'effacement'.[44]

Yet the principles of courtly love underlie many traditional as well as recent theoretical descriptions of literary production. Whether the players be the theorist and his 'Other' or the poet and his muse, the game is one of sexual politics. In imaginative literature, this game has a rich and expressive history. The poet is the quester and the lover, and the woman is his inspiration and the object of his desire. As Plato explains: 'the Muse first of all inspires men herself.'[45] In Renaissance and Romantic literature this association of woman with the muse is strengthened. Whether the figure is Beatrice or Laura, Lucy or Emily, it is she who draws the poet's imagination in love and ambition to gain her. That she is distant, mysterious, hard to win or simply dead is a characteristic requirement of that imagination. The muse must carefully regulate the economy of the poet's desire to win her and his desire to be still writing about her.

The ease with which Harold Bloom connects the Freudian Oedipal drama with a revived mythology of the muse shows how long-lived and persistent this mythology is. Like Freud's theory of the Oedipal complex, on which he founds 'the beginnings of religion, morals, society, and art'[46] in *Totem and Taboo*, Bloom's large theory of influence is based on a primal strife between fathers and sons for the acquisition of the woman as object. 'In the wholeness of the poet's imagination,' he declares, 'the Muse is mother and harlot at once.' The imaginative enterprise of the new young poet is then to wrest this muse from his father 'precursors'.[47] As a number of feminist critics have pointed out,[48] this large-scale theory of creative influence delegates gender roles with high insouciance. In it, women have no part as writers or poets themselves. They are ascribed the lofty status of the muse entirely for the benefit of a patrilineal succession. That Bloom can draw eclectic support from such writers as St Paul, Vico, Rousseau, Kierkegaard, Nietzsche, Freud and Lacan, for instance, is a sign of how powerful and coherent a tradition of thought lies behind his own 'family romance'[49] of creativity.

It is this very authority by exclusion which marks the weak point of such theories, in so far as they might be used as theories of women's writing. Their very rigid ascription of roles beggars their own relevance in literary criticism. The woman who writes cannot be a muse or an 'Other', and she ceases to be an object of mystery or desire. Instead, she assumes the new power of being a subject in her own right, but in a tradition which has no mythological or ideological description for that subjectivity. She is an anomaly, a usurper. She is fated to remain unaccountable. The very strength and prevalence of theories of writing which relegate woman to the role of 'Other' certainly reveal the odds against which any particular woman must seek to account for herself as a writer. In the nineteenth century these odds were even more heavily loaded against women who presumed to write.

In *A Vindication of the Rights of Woman*, Mary Wollstonecraft quotes a curious anecdote from Rousseau's *Émile*. Rousseau gives the example of one young girl who would play at writing the letter 'O' with her needle before she had been taught to use a pen. However, he tells, one day 'she happened to see herself in the looking-glass', and was so shocked at her unbecoming appearance in 'the constrained attitude'[50] of writing, that she determined never to attempt to write

20

again. This idea of a mirror-stage which interrupts the girl's concentration with self-consciousness is offered as proof of the natural intellectual inferiority of women. It is a stronger proof, however, of the predilections of the author. The familiar opposition of womanliness and genius, of grace and strength, of muse and poet, is at work in Rousseau's example. By taking up a makeshift pen and trying to write for herself, the girl threatens to deprive her observer of a desirable, inspiring image in the mirror. It is *his* distaste for her 'constrained attitude' which, one suspects, dictates her return to her needlework. Rousseau claims to prove the point that it is a girl's natural state to be pretty, graceful and self-conscious. But the message he betrays is that he fears to lose her services in the role of a muse—he fears to lose the graceful figure in the mirror.

Robert Graves, in *The White Goddess*, brings together many myths of creativity, and finely summarises their drift when he asserts that, 'woman is not a poet: she is either a Muse or she is nothing.'[51] This rigid allocation of roles, he admits, cannot hide the fact that some women have been poets.[52] But the work charts a long and continuing history of denying women a rightful description of their creativity and of their own strategies with regard to the muse. 'I'm a woman, sir' (VIII, 1130), Aurora Leigh declares in triumphant self-assertion at the end of her poem. That assertiveness, however, has to be learned in a slow, difficult, lonely struggle against a tradition which denies her any natural description of herself as a poet. It is not, then, enough to ask of Barrett Browning, 'Does she have a muse, and what is its sex?'[53] One must also ask, what is the relation of the muse to this woman's writing?

Against the gender prescriptiveness of much recent theory, Margaret Homans urges that 'it was just as

21

important for a woman to find a substitute for her father or brother as it was for a man to displace mother or sister.'[54] It is not in Barrett Browning's political views or in some special property of her language that her difference as a woman poet is to be found. It is rather in that assertion of her right to speak, which runs throughout her poems, and which must be won both from the mirror which would reflect her as an object merely, and from the figure who above all inspires and threatens, with his own, natural, inherited power, her sense of herself as a poet. For Barrett Browning, it is the father who stands for that 'Other' against which her poetry shapes itself and grows strong. The politics of her relation to him are therefore essentially different from those which govern the male poet and his muse, and they ask for a different account.

Chapter Two

'No name . . . My father! more belov'd than *thine*!': The Daughter's First Muse

> For 'neath thy gentleness of praise,
> My Father! rose my early lays!
> And when the lyre was scarce awake,
> I lov'd its strings for *thy* lov'd sake;
> Woo'd the kind Muses—but the while
> Thought only how to win thy smile—
> ('To My Father on His Birthday', 33–8)[1]

The story of Mr Barrett's emotional and financial domination of his family is well known. It was not only his favourite oldest daughter, but all his eleven children who suffered from the extraordinary rigidity of his rule against marriage. There was, Elizabeth reports, a regular 'setting forth of the whole doctrine', which was a doctrine of ' "passive obedience, & particularly in respect to marriage" '. This uncompromising 'monomania' (*Letters: 1845–1846*, I, 408) forced her, at the age of forty, into a secret marriage with Robert Browning, and subsequent escape from her father's house to Italy. Her worst fears about his reactions were well founded. Mr Barrett

23

refused to communicate further with his once best-loved daughter. He had all her belongings removed from the house, and years later returned her many pleading letters, unopened. He died in 1857, apparently unrepentant of this strange rule of law, and unshaken by the fact that three of his children, Elizabeth, Henrietta and George, had eloped and been disinherited in his lifetime.

The psychological and emotional explanations for this story have long been the material of biographies, and the reputation of Barrett Browning in the twentieth century rests largely on the intriguing resonances of this story. Thus, for instance, *The Barretts of Wimpole Street* relishes the idea of an incestuous element in the relationship of father and daughter, and finds piquant evidence for it in their shared night prayers, as well as in that prolonged invalidism which made Elizabeth so flatteringly dependent. Virginia Woolf endorses such an interpretation in *Three Guineas*, where she describes Mr Barrett as the worst example of the 'infantile fixation'[2] of many Victorian fathers, of whom her own father, of course, provided another powerful example. More recent biographies have tried to find extenuating reasons for this obsessive despotism, in Mr Barrett's acute loneliness after the death of his wife,[3] for instance, and in the possibility that he turned wholly to his young, adoring children for emotional compensation.[4] That he was much loved and admired seems indisputable, and the many birthday odes written for him with playful grandiloquence by his children are a sign of it. One of Elizabeth's own tributes, 'To My Father on His Birthday' (1826), amply acknowledges his power to inspire her love and to make all other loves seem poor by comparison. The 'name' of that father was, from an early age, more 'belov'd' than any other.

But the poem also acknowledges his power to inspire

her writing. The emotional domination of the father was inseparable from his imaginative attraction and authority. The young poet remembers how she 'Woo'd the kind Muses', but in reality 'Thought only how to win thy smile.' The traditional female sources of inspiration were early supplanted by the figure of her uniquely adored father. The power of that father's 'smile' did not then lessen with time, but continued to be, throughout the poet's life, a figure for the only imaginative reward she cared to seek and feared to lose. Consequently, it is important to recognise that the other side of the story of Mr Barrett's 'infantile fixation' and quirks of tyranny is to be found in some profound and lasting need in the daughter for that very paternal power which he exercised with such convinced righteousness. Her poetry registers the strength of that need almost to the end of her life.

However, Barrett Browning's private emotional and literary dedication to her father must also be seen in the context of a larger seductive ideology of fatherhood, which predominated in the nineteenth century, and which was particularly strong in the writings of Victorian women. As Elaine Showalter points out, a common trait among women writers of the century was their 'identification with, and dependence upon, the father; and either loss of, or alienation from, the mother.'[5] By contrast to the mother's constant association with childbearing and death, the father's free physical strength must have seemed enviably the superior lot. Furthermore, as de Beauvoir notes, the father's access to a life outside the home gave him a 'mysterious prestige',[6] a glamour of freedom and worldly wisdom, in the emulous imagination of the daughter.

As a result, there develops round the figure of the father in nineteenth-century literature a very persuasive myth of power, knowledge and reliability. It is a myth which the socially dependent but ambitious daughter has her reasons to perpetuate. The father's superior education and freedom of movement are both privileges which she desires for herself, if not literally, at least imaginatively. He is the sign of a power to be envied, courted and gained. However, the social and moral authority of the father is also a force which prohibits the daughter from seeking too much knowledge, freedom or power of her own. While he is, on the one hand, a sign of what the daughter desires for herself, he is also, on the other hand, a sign that restricts her desires. This contradiction forcefully shapes her attitude to him.

Elizabeth Barrett would have found corroboration for her own emotional idealisation of her father in a book she read many times and which profoundly influenced her poetry. 'I have read *Corinne* for the third time . . . It is an immortal book' (*Boyd*, p.176), she wrote at the age of twenty-six. Madame de Staël's *Corinne*, as Ellen Moers has shown,[7] influenced a whole generation of women, and encouraged a widespread fantasy of the woman as dedicated artist who forfeits love for her ambition. However, there is another aspect of *Corinne* which might have endeared it to the female imagination at this time: namely, its consciousness of the power of the father. Madame de Staël's attitude to her own father was one of curiously uninhibited sentimental and sexual attraction. 'Of all the men in the world it is he I would have wished for a lover,'[8] she declared at the age of nineteen, and after his death, she lamented him in equally passionate terms: 'I was to lose my protector, my father, my brother, my friend, he whom I would have chosen to be the only love of my life if fate had not cast me in a generation other than his.'[9]

The strange fact behind this lifelong adoration is that de Staël's father disapproved of her writing. *Corinne* was written immediately after his death, and is, on the one hand, a loving commemoration of him. But it is also, on the other hand, a guilt-ridden story of betrayal. The hero, Lord Nelvil, is haunted by the memory of his dead father's wish that he should marry, not the passionate, artistic, Italian Corinne, but the quiet, domesticated, English Lucile. His love for Corinne therefore carries a disproportionate and irredeemable load of guilt, that is not only guilt of betraying the beloved father, but of betraying a whole array of powers which the father represents: 'j'avais trahi sa tendresse, et . . . j'étais rebelle à ma patrie, à la volonté paternelle, à tout ce qu'il y a de sacré sur la terre'[10] (I had betrayed his tender love, and . . . I was a rebel against my country, against the paternal will, against everything that is sacred on earth). Although *Corinne*, on the one hand, shows the triumph of the woman as artist, it also, on the other hand, shows the triumph of the paternal will and of filial love. 'Je n'ai jamais rien aimé plus profondément que mon père'[11] (I have loved nothing more deeply than my father), the hero declares. That love is the real emotional centre of the novel. It is as if de Staël were expiating her own guilt of writing against her father's will by having her hero finally adhere to his dead father's wishes. However, the fact that the two themes of woman's ambition and of filial love are separated in the novel betrays the extent to which they represent a contradiction of purpose in the author. De Staël's insistence on passive obedience to the father on the one hand and total independence for the woman artist on the other reveals her essentially female conflict of desire.

The enormous popularity of *Corinne* among nineteenth-century women writers may have derived, not only from its celebration of the woman as artist and its eulogies of Italy as the place of artistic and sexual freedom, but also from its troubled portrayal of the power of the dead father. The time-honoured story of romantic love as an escape from parental tyranny is complicated, here, by a rival love between father and son. That it is really a love between father and daughter is a secret that the novel fails to keep. It seems unlikely that Elizabeth Barrett, who marked all those passages in her copy of *Oedipus at Colonus*, for instance, where Antigone warmly declares her love for her father,[12] did not note and appreciate the powerful myth of the father which broods through *Corinne* and determines, both emotionally and literally, the outcome of its plot.

> My beloved father has gone away . . . His tears fell almost as fast as mine did when we parted . . . I never told him of it, of course, but, when I was last so ill, I used to start out of fragments of dreams, broken from all parts of the universe, with the cry from my own lips, 'Oh, Papa, Papa!' I could not trace it back to the dream behind, yet there it always was very curiously, and touchingly too, to my own heart, seeming scarcely *of* me, though it came *from* me, at once waking me with, and welcoming me to, the old straight humanities. (*MRM*, I, 104)

Elizabeth Barrett wrote this while recuperating in Torquay in 1838. She was thirty-two years old. Such expressions of demonstrative reliance on her father recur throughout her early letters. Although probably exaggerated by illness, her automatic call for ' "Papa" ' from the midst of her hectic dreams shows how deeply her consciousness has imbibed the idea of his moral dependability. Simply the invocation of his name can banish the terrors of her sleep. He is a source of sanity and restraint, and a reminder of 'the old straight humanities.' This myth of protectiveness and moral authority which her imagination builds round the name of her father draws on a strong and uninhibited emotional connection between them: 'His tears fell almost as fast as mine did . . . ' The myth is strengthened by the emotional intensity of a relation which often seems to poach the language of sexual love without any sense of indecorum. The 'beloved father' weeps almost as unrestrainedly as his daughter at parting.

Certainly, Elizabeth Barrett would not have been surprised at the sentiments voiced by George Eliot about nursing her father through his last illness. The young Marian Evans wrote that 'these will ever be the happiest days of life to me. The one deep strong love I have ever known has now its highest exercise and fullest reward.' In another letter she goes on to stress the moral security offered by her father: 'What shall I be without my Father? It will seem as if a part of my moral nature were gone. I had a horrid vision of myself last night becoming earthly sensual and devilish for want of that purifying restraining influence.'[13] In both passages, the daughter's emotionally demonstrative love for the father is closely linked with a sense of his moral authority. The father is a rescue from a state of encroaching mental confusion or moral anarchy. He saves his daughter from the terrors of her own dreams or from the terrors of her own dangerous proclivities to be 'earthly sensual devilish'. It is as if the figure of the father, by freeing and then channelling the daughter's expressions of love towards himself, thus protects her from the alternative forbidden expression of her feelings. This law of the father is one which prohibits the daughter's desires precisely by permitting her 'one deep strong love' for himself.

The association of the father's emotional accessibility

with a moral law is evident in Barrett Browning's writing as it is in de Staël's and George Eliot's. The consequence, however, is that the father saves his daughter not only from herself, but also from the moral threat that comes from other men. The sense of him as an alternative is still strong in those letters Barrett Browning wrote after her marriage. 'Always he has had the greatest power over my heart,' she wrote some weeks after her arrival in Italy—not of Robert but of her father—'because I am of those weak women who reverence strong men. By a word he might have bound me to him hand and foot' (*Kenyon*, I, 291). She admits here, startlingly, that if her father had returned her love, she could not have left him. He alone possessed a natural 'power' over her 'heart'. Even after the romance and happiness of her marriage, the idea of that 'power' continued to press upon her imagination with the force, not only of a tyrannical rule which she had shed, but also of a love which she had lost.

Simone de Beauvoir, in *The Second Sex*, might be commenting on Barrett Browning in particular when she writes: 'If her father shows affection for his daughter, she feels that her existence is magnificently justified . . . she is fulfilled and deified. All her life she may longingly seek that lost state of plenitude and peace.'[14] The father appears in Barrett Browning's poetry as the object of that quest for inspiration and power which all her life she pursues. But he also represents a 'power' which can bind her 'hand and foot'. To seek the father 'longingly,' as she might the 'lost state of plenitude and peace' that womanhood has forgone, is also to seek, however, a crippling dependence and powerlessness for herself. Her theory of creativity is one which, throughout her life, is closely implicated with the power of the father as something she desires to keep, but needs to repudiate. The emotional attraction and the ideological danger of that power are the contradictory but linked aspects of the figure whose 'smile' supplants all the other 'kind Muses'.

In 'To My Father on His Birthday' the young poet had written:

> But still my Father's looks remain
> The best Maecenas of my strain;
> My gentlest joy, upon his brow
> To read the smile, that meets me now—
>
> (43–6)

Nearly twenty years later, Elizabeth Barrett, at the age of thirty eight, lovingly dedicated her 1844 collection of poetry to her father. She invoked his attention and his approval with the words: *'it is my fancy thus to seem to return to a visible personal dependence on you, as if indeed I were a child again; to conjure your beloved image between myself and the public, so as to be sure of one smile . . '*.[15] This Dedication was Elizabeth's last to her father. A month or so after its publication she received her first letter from Robert Browning. Nonetheless, the thought of that potent 'smile' continued to haunt her for the rest of her life. Two years after her marriage, for instance, and after the disappointment of another miscarriage, she wrote to Miss Mitford that 'perhaps after all . . . I should choose the smile of my own father to that of my own child . . . oh yes, I should & would' (*MRM*, III, 234). That her father might smile on her was still the goal of her ambition and the end of her desires.

This lifelong and single-minded courtship of the figure of her father neatly endorses recent feminist descriptions of the woman poet's relation to her muse. While the task of 'the strong poet', according to Harold Bloom, is to ' "rescue" the beloved Muse from his

31

precursors',[16] the task of the strong female poet, as Gilbert and Gubar emphasise,[17] must be different. This difference is persuasively analysed by Joanne Feit Diehl, who argues that poets like Christina Rossetti, Barrett Browning and Emily Dickinson do not distinguish between precursor and muse in this way, but rather look back to a single, composite precursor-muse figure which is male.[18] This general father-lover then stands in a difficult, exclusive relation to the female poet. He is both desired and threatening—desired like the muse, but threatening because he wields a power the daughter desires for herself. Thus the very fact of courting the father's appreciation risks upsetting the natural hierarchy of their relation. For Barrett Browning, the contradiction which informs her imagination's myth of the father is the contradiction of wanting to be to him both a daughter and a strong poet; of wanting, as she writes in the 1844 Dedication, *'to satisfy my heart while I sanctify my ambition'*. The many poems that invoke the presence of the father reveal the extent to which this contradiction shaped her identity as a poet.

'A Romance of the Ganges' (1838) is one of a number of ballads which Elizabeth Barrett wrote in response to a demand in the 1830s and 1840s for morally educative poems, which were published in illustrated annuals and were directed towards a primarily female readership. Her own contributions were generally highly-coloured tales of tragically thwarted romantic love, ending in death or suicide. But the moral of these, however coy and high-minded it might sound, is often curiously obfuscated by the presence of a father or a mother. It is this confusion of purpose which makes these early ballads unexpectedly interesting.

'A Romance of the Ganges' was written to illustrate a picture of ' "a very charming group of Hindoo girls floating their lamps upon the Ganges" ' (*MRM*, I, 37, note 2), as Miss Mitford explained, and was published in the annual which she edited, and which carried the alluring title of *Findens' Tableaux of the Affections: a Series of Picturesque Illustrations of the Womanly Virtues*. It tells the story of two girls, Luti and Nuleeni. Luti has lost her lover to Nuleeni, and as proof of it the lamp on her boat goes out. In anger, she exacts from the younger girl a vow that, once married, she will remind her husband of his faithlessness to her friend. So far, it is a picturesque tale of spoilt love. But there is a third presence in the poem, for which there is no original in Miss Mitford's ' "charming" ' picture.

Luti remembers that by this same river of love she had sat with her dying father. Furthermore, she remembers the highly suggestive fact that ' "on my childish knee was leaned/My dying father's head" ' (75-6).[19] This memory provides Luti with a strong alternative to the love she has lost. She declares: ' "I weep no faithless lover where/I wept a loving father" ' (88-9). As in *Corinne*, the figure of the dead father exerts a compelling emotional hold over the actions of his child. Faithful paternal love is contrasted with faithless romantic love, and Luti determines, therefore, to be constant to the first.

However, the troubling fact remains that the father is dead. He is faithful but lost, so that the daughter's choice of romantic or paternal love involves a choice of life or death. The poem's finale has all the narrative predictability of a tale of thwarted love. But the moral is confusing. Luti drowns herself, not because the lover was treacherous, but because the father was constant. The adult daughter kills herself in order to be faithful to the memory of the father's love which she had known as a child. It is to the poem's credit, at least, that in the end it remains unclear which of '*the Womanly Virtues*' is being illustrated.

In fact, 'A Romance of the Ganges' is not about womanly virtues at all. It is about an emotional rivalry that looms large in the consciousness of the daughter. Father and lover are forces that contend for her love, and of the two she chooses her father. However, the poem also subtly undermines the validity of this choice. The father offers a secure primal faithfulness, but he offers it in death. The picture of the child nursing and supporting her dying father suggests a connection which is not just the connection of a somehow acceptable emotional and even erotic experience—the experience George Eliot described as the 'highest exercise and fullest reward' of her 'one deep strong love'. There is another more sinister connection in this picture, which will haunt Barrett Browning's imagination throughout her life. This connection becomes clear in a subsequent ballad, written a year later, in 1839.

Elizabeth Barrett sent 'The Lay of the Brown Rosary' (1844), which she termed a 'Patagonian ballad', and an 'ichthyosaurus of a ballad' (MRM, I, 135), with some justified trepidation to Miss Mitford. The poem is a female re-working of the Faust myth. Onora, the heroine, sells her soul to the ghostly nun of the brown rosary in order to repeal a divine decree that she must die. Thus she hopes to be able to marry her betrothed. This queer moral premise purports to show Onora foolishly bartering immortal life for earthly love. But punishment is exacted on the very altar steps at her wedding, when her lover falls dead at her feet. After this, Onora herself pines away and dies. However, Elizabeth Barrett brings to this improbable Gothic tale an idea which radically confuses the romantic impulse of the story. This is, once again, the idea of the dead father.

Onora, we are told, consorts with the ghost of a nun who was ' "buried alive" ' (46)[20] for some sin against her vow; of course, her vow of chastity. But unlike *Villette*, where the nun will represent Lucy's bid for freedom and sexual love, here the nun is an evil spirit who has designs on the heroine's immortal soul. What is strange, however, is that there is no social or even religious basis for the divine decree that Onora should die rather than marry. The lover is approved of by her family, and he is honourable. Thus the usual justifications for a social or familial prohibition are missing. This is not a case of illicit or immoral love, from which Onora might be protected by authoritative moral forces. It is simply a case of her not being permitted to love at all. The reasons for this ruthlessly prohibitive story are to be found in a third shadowy presence in the poem.

At one point Onora has a dream. 'I only walk among the fields, beneath the autumn-sun,/With my dead father, hand in hand, as I have often done' (137–8), she relates. Against the powers of evil, represented by the nun and the earthly lover, there are ranged the powers of good, represented by Onora's family, and especially by her dead father. This distribution of moral forces in the poem means that the family is on the side of God's decree that Onora must die, unwed. However, the absurdity of this moral alignment is blurred by something else in the poem: 'And then he calleth through my dreams, he calleth tenderly,/"Come forth, my daughter, my beloved, and walk the fields with me!"' (144–5). Onora's dreams of her good father are dreams that reveal an alternative motive for the poem's odd construction. With the figure of the father, there is introduced an emotional charge which radically displaces the moral of the story. '"Come forth, my daughter, my beloved, and walk the fields with me!"' is a call that sounds as emotionally compelling as any earthly lover's. The father calls his daughter, like Solomon calling his ' "beloved" '. It is this connection between the dead father and the unwed daughter that carries the conviction which is plainly missing from the narrative and moral structure of the poem. God's decree is justified by the dead father's infinitely compelling and desirable love.

However, in her response to that father's lover-like call, Onora implicitly acknowledges the conditions of that love:

> Have patience, O dead father mine! I did not fear to die—
> I wish I were a young dead child and had thy company!
> I wish I lay beside thy feet, a buried three-year child,
> And wearing only a kiss of thine upon my lips that smiled!
> (162–5)

These lines are like Elizabeth Barrett's own words of Dedication to her father: *'it is my fancy thus to seem to return to a visible personal dependence on you, as if indeed I were a child again.'* Onora's dream of being a child again is also, however, a dream of being dead. It is as if Elizabeth Barrett were here obscurely remembering another 'three-year child' who stayed faithful by dying: the child Lucy. Wordsworth's desire to retain his imagination's 'memory of what has been,/And never more will be' (41–2)[21] requires the sacrifice of Lucy to nature's amorous but deadly ways. Onora's reply suggests that the crime from which she must be saved is not that of over-reaching Faustian desire, nor of illicit love, nor of consorting with evil spirits; her crime is simply the fact of having become a woman, and of having betrayed the father's love with other kisses on her lips. This is the reason why she must die, and why she herself really wishes to have died. She imagines staying in a prelapsarian world of childhood, and walking with her father there, 'hand in hand'. But it is not just childhood which this belated, post-Romantic daughter desires; it is a permanent childhood, and therefore a childhood sealed by death. Onora's strange concealed guilt, in this poem, is the guilt of having lived on.

The figure of the dead father, then, is the key to the hidden message of these confused and precipitate ballads. The father is dead, not by some sad chance, but *because* the daughter lives. The connection between the father's death and the daughter's life is a profoundly suggestive and influential one, which in both poems sanctions the suicidal direction of the ending. The daughter forgoes earthly love in order to answer the more seductive call of the dead father who offers her, instead, a lasting security and dependency. He offers her her childhood once again. Such a call implicitly, therefore, requires the daughter to deny her adult self; it requires a permanent stalling of her development into womanhood. To be *'as if indeed . . . a child again'* is the main emotional impetus behind these surprising romances.

It is possible to detect in these poems the beginning of a contradiction in Elizabeth Barrett's attitude. The father's emotional attraction is one which distorts all morality and all logic. In 'The Lay of the Brown Rosary' it is he who gives emotional validity to the decree that Onora must not live on and love, and who thus sides with God in making her other desires sinful. The idea that the father is a source of moral security and constancy entails the idea that he prohibits the daughter's own chaotic or sensual desires. But to prohibit them entirely is to command the daughter's suicide. ' "Come forth, my daughter, my beloved, and walk the fields with me!" ' is tender only to disguise a paternal fiat that is, like God's, tyrannically absolute for the daughter's death.

These poems seem to proclaim that the father's love

triumphs over all others, and that the daughter finds the 'lost state of plenitude and peace' of her childhood's dependence on him, by dying before being wed. Nonetheless, they also proclaim that to reach such love and such emotional plenitude the daughter must no longer live or love others. The unmentioned third prohibition, implicitly commanded by the father's otherworldly possessiveness, is that she should no longer write either. That both ballads end in the daughter's suicide or death is a comment which cannot entirely ride on the justification of emotional constancy. To die still a child to the father is to renounce more than the loves which threaten his; it is to renounce the power of writing also. It is that consciousness of power which is indicatively lacking in these ballads, but which, when it is present, creates a conflict of purpose that lies at the heart of Barrett Browning's father-centred poetics.

'But dear Papa's wishes w.d be consulted more tenderly, if his commands were less straight & absolute' (*MRM*, III, 129), Elizabeth wrote in 1845, with a noticeable new uncertainty in her tone. Throughout the letters written to Robert in 1845 and 1846 it is possible to detect a struggle to believe still in the old cherished ideal of her father. But while she had once proclaimed that 'my poor most beloved Papa's *biases* are sacred to me' (*MRM*, I, 226), she now tells Robert of how every member of her family, except herself, is humiliatingly 'dependent in money-matters on the inflexible will'. That 'will', which she had once looked to as a moral authority, and which she had deified as near to God's, now comes to seem 'inflexible'. But, she adds anxiously, 'what you do NOT see what you *cannot* see, is the deep tender affection behind & below all those patriarchal ideas of governing grownup children' (*Letters: 1845–1846*, I, 169). Her faith in that 'deep tender affection' might still excuse and mitigate her father's 'patriarchal ideas of governing'.

But it is evident in these letters that the dear ideal of her father is under threat from two figures associated with it. Just as in 'The Lay of the Brown Rosary' the father sides with the divine decree that the daughter must die, so in these letters the father's will seems sometimes harsh as God's. He is the 'High priest' (*MRM*, III, 127) and 'grand Signor' (*MRM*, III, 129) of the household, and, as Elizabeth knew well, his 'principle of passive filial obedience' was 'held . . drawn (& quartered) from Scripture' (*Letters: 1845–1846*, I, 408). Mr Barrett ruled his children with the convinced authority of a Jehovah.

But there was another figure which Elizabeth came to associate, however reluctantly, with her father. 'I belong to a family of West Indian slaveholders, and if I believed in curses, I should be afraid' (*Kenyon*, II, 220), she once reported. Mr Barrett owned sugar plantations in Jamaica until the Abolition in 1833, when he lost much of his wealth. The idea of slavery is one which creeps into Elizabeth's descriptions of her father's rule, though she never accuses him directly of using the tactics of a slave-owner. His 'principle of passive filial obedience,' for instance, is one which encourages in his children that 'disingenuousness' and 'cowardice' which she calls the '"vices of slaves"' (*Letters: 1845–1846*, I, 169). Elsewhere, she describes to Robert one of those domestic scenes in which all the children 'walked out of the room' leaving only the suitor of Henrietta to hear the end of the lecture on '"passive obedience."' She reports, without comment, that at the end Captain Surtees Cook asked '"if children were to be considered slaves"' (*Letters: 1845–1846*, I, 408–9). That the 'essential features' of the patriarchal family are 'the incorporation of unfree persons and paternal power'[22] was a knowledge stressed by the facts of the family inheritance, but also by Elizabeth's own reluctant perceptions. It was only after her marriage in 1846 that she was able to write a poem which powerfully repudiates the authority which had so magisterially dominated her own life.

'The Runaway Slave at Pilgrim's Point' (1850) tells the story of a nameless female slave, who has seen her black lover killed by white masters, and who has herself been raped by them. To her horror, she subsequently bears a white child. The language of the whole poem is marked by the ideological division of black and white: black slaves and white masters, black mother and white child, black earth and white heaven. There is no moral authority which can be exempted from this stark new relativism of a world seen black or white. Even the authority of God is implicated, for he comes with incriminatingly 'fine white angels' (157).[23] In spite of all its heightened melodrama and carrying rhetoric, 'The Runaway Slave' is still a startlingly iconoclastic poem. This is because it breaks with two sacred myths of English Victorian society: the myths of motherhood and fatherhood.

At one point the slave looks on her child and sees that he is white:

> My own, own child! I could not bear
>   To look in his face, it was so white;
> I covered him up with a kerchief there,
>   I covered his face in close and tight:
> And he moaned and struggled, as well might be,
> For the white child wanted his liberty—
>   Ha, ha! he wanted the master-right.
>
>   (120–6)

The new moral order is simply one of white and black,

and even the prototypically innocent child cannot escape it. The imperialism of whiteness is a hereditary one, and the child's desire for liberty is a desire already corrupted by the assumption of 'master-right'. Because the system of master and slave is based on an original birthright, there is only one course of defiance for the female slave:

> Why, in that single glance I had
>   Of my child's face, . . . I tell you all,
> I saw a look that made me mad!
>   The *master's* look, that used to fall
> On my soul like his lash . . . or worse!
> And so, to save it from my curse,
>   I twisted it round in my shawl.
>
> (141–7)

The easiness of this last verb neatly avoids any note of tragedy or sentimentality. The logic of killing the child comes as naturally as wrapping it in a shawl for protection. Simply by the fact of its colour, and to some extent, one imagines, of its sex, the white child inherits the *'master's* look'. The only way to break this imperial lineage is quietly to kill him, and the poem accomplishes the black slave's revolt with persuasive moral conviction.

However, this is a poem which protests not only at the domination of black races by white, but also at the domination that is carried out in the name of the *father*. The rape of the black slave is an outrage which is perfectly consistent with the myth of power that supports the rule of the white masters. The child inherits the father's look as well as the master's. The mystique of the father's line and of the father's name is one which the poem questions and defies. It shows fatherhood in complicity with racial power, and the sign

41

of both lies in the authority of the 'name'. That 'name' stands for mastery, and its repetition creates in the poem a linguistic line of descent which links fathers of all kinds in a league of power which naturally excludes the nameless female slave herself.

At the start, she kneels where the first Pilgrim Fathers landed and where they thanked their God 'for liberty' (4):

> O pilgrims, I have gasped and run
> All night long from the whips of one
>   Who in your names works sin and woe!
>   (12–14)

The 'names' of those first Fathers are the origin of a long history of 'sin and woe'—a history which leads logically to the act of violent fathering that is perpetrated in the poem's story. Along this route is to be found also *God the Father*:

> Indeed we live beneath the sky,
>   That great smooth Hand of God stretched out
> On all His children fatherly . . .
>   (43–5)

This divine father is soon found to be partisan for the white man. He has thrown the black race 'Under the feet of His white creatures' (26), and he comes equipped with his own 'fine white angels' (157). This patrilineal succession is a white succession, and it is one that links all white fathers both divine and human.

However, there is an alternative name in the poem, which the black slave chants like a spell. It is the name of her black lover:

> I sang his name instead of a song,

42

Over and over I sang his name,
Upward and downward I drew it along
My various notes,—the same, the same!

(78–81)

Significantly, this is the 'name' of what might be a
different succession—a line fathered by love and
rebellion rather than hatred and domination. But such a
'name' cannot belong to the white child: 'I dared not sing
to the white-faced child/ The only song I knew' (132–3).
The white child already carries in the colour of his skin
the 'name' of his authority and mastery. There is no
humanitarian solution in this poem to the system of
power by birthright. There is only the possibility of
breaking the system, by killing the child who will bear
the name of a long line of fathers: the first Pilgrim
Fathers and 'their hunter sons' (204). Such language is
explicit. This is a rule of fathers and sons, and the black
woman can only refuse to perpetuate it. She buries the
white child in the black earth, and immediately she is
free again to sing the other 'name': 'I sate down smiling
there and sung/ The song I learnt in my maidenhood'
(188–9).

The name of the father is thus, on the one hand, the
sign of inherited right to power. But it is also, on the
other hand, a principle of inspiration. The slave sings her
black lover's 'name instead of a song', and it remains,
behind all her 'various notes,' simply 'the same, the
same!' This idea of the name as an external source of
creative power is one which recurs in Barrett Browning's
verse, and in 'The Runaway Slave' it glancingly suggests
a theory of poetry in which the man's name is needed to
steady the woman's words. The name of the lover is the
raison d'être of the woman's love-song, but it remains
secret in order that the song should go on. This need for

the one name behind all common names is expressed in one of the *Sonnets from the Portuguese*, for instance, where Elizabeth Barrett writes:

> And this . . . this lute and song . . . loved yesterday,
> (The singing angels know) are only dear
> Because thy name moves right in what they say.
>
> (Sonnet VII)[24]

Poetry is authorised by the one 'name' which might put an end to all naming if it were spoken, but which, unspoken, is like a muse, drawing the poet's words in desire towards itself.

However, in Barrett Browning's imagination, the name which holds her in its power and which she more often sings is that of the father. 'The Runaway Slave' rejects the name of the line of white fathers, and would supplant it with the name of the lover, thus implicitly reversing the romance of the earlier ballads. But in many other poems, which have not the political guilt and the personal freedom of this one, the daughter's creativity needs the name of the father to give authority to her verse. 'No name can e'er on tablet shine,/ My father! more belov'd than *thine*!' (11–12). This early personal declaration of dependence in 'To My Father on His Birthday' is never fully revoked. But it is never again so gladly celebrated. That fatherhood is a sign which supports a religious and political imperialism is a fact which Barrett Browning knows and forcefully condemns. But that it is a sign of creative power which the daughter admires and envies is a fact with which she must continue to struggle.

'Papa would laugh at me if he stood near; he who always laughs whenever I say "I am busy,"—laughs like Jove with superior amusement. As if people could

44

possibly be busy with rhymes . . . ' (*Horne*, II, 284).
Although she courted her father's attention and her
father's smile as the reward of her writing, it seems that
Mr Barrett had little appreciation of his daughter's
poems, and that he was often inclined to laugh at her.
Yet, that he 'laughs like Jove' suggests something also of
the attraction of his power. He remains a high god in his
very aloofness and mockery. He is the philistine and
thunderous Jove, who must be continually supplicated
and won. Like some authoritarian, unbending muse, he
inspires constant effort in order to be moved. His smile is
hard to gain. But more often than his smile, it is that
other characteristic of his nature which awaits the
daughter poet: his thunder.

'Only one person holds the thunder—& I shall be
thundered at; I shall not be reasoned with' (*Letters:
1845–1846*, I, 318–19), Elizabeth wrote in trepidation to
Robert, on hearing his proposal to confront her father
with the truth about his love for her. On another
occasion her fear of that thunder proved justified when
Mr Barrett, discovering that Robert's visit had been
prolonged during a storm, furiously admonished his
daughter, and looked, to her, all the time 'as if the
thunder had passed into him' (*Letters: 1845–1846*, II, 922).
He could seem the very incarnation of that elemental
energy to which she was so nervously sensitive. 'I never
wait to enquire whether it thunders to the left or the
right, to be frightened most ingloriously' (*Letters:
1845–1846*, I, 119), she confided to Robert. One of her
rare memories of her mother is of a 'sweet, gentle
nature, which the thunder a little turned from its
sweetness' (*Letters: 1845–1846*, II, 1012). The high
prerogative of Jove is not only to laugh at small things
'with superior amusement', but also to spoil or destroy
them with his thunderbolt.

45

Yet, in spite of her constitutional terror of storms and in spite of her abhorrence of the moral violence of her father, Barrett Browning, as a poet, is intrigued and envious of the power he wields. His name and his thunder are signs of an authority which, imaginatively, she desires to make her own. The power of the creator-god is like the power of the Romantic poet. In both cases, it is associated with the thunder and lightning of the storm. The daughter poet's desire for her father is not only a desire to court his smile or speak his name; it is also a desire to overcome her fear and steal his thunder.

'The Tempest' (1833) is an early poem, based on an actual storm which occurred in 1826. Elizabeth Barrett wrote it in her twenties. However, the differences between the storm which she describes in a letter and the events of the poem are interesting. In the original storm, the young poet stood transfixed at the window, from where she witnessed the lightning strike a large old tree, 'within two hundred yards' of where she was standing. Some time later, news reached her of the deaths of 'two young women' (*Letters: 1845-1846*, I, 119-20) who had also been struck. In 'The Tempest', however, she makes some strategic changes. First, the speaker goes out into the storm and rejoices in its violence; secondly, the two women are replaced by a single male character; and thirdly, this victim becomes mysteriously known to the speaker. There is thus an emotional nexus in the poem which is new, and which is both startlingly intimate and tantalisingly unspecific. This has led critics to suggest that 'The Tempest' is a highly autobiographical poem, and that the male victim of the storm is Elizabeth's beloved brother Edward,[25] or else her father.[26] The theme and imagery point strongly to the latter. It was her father's fanciful, metal-spired house, Hope End, which seemed to Elizabeth designed to attract all the lightnings of heaven. She associated that father, throughout her life, with the thunderous and violent god Jove. Furthermore, it was that same father who looked with scorn and impatience on her own fear of storms, and who thus seemed to put into question her Romantic 'pretension to poetry' (*Letters: 1845–1846*, I, 119). The evidence of the letters suggests that the imagery of thunder and lightning was often linked in Elizabeth's mind with the thought of her godly, authoritative father.

However, 'The Tempest' is interesting, not just because it seems to enact a private drama of revenge, but because it enacts an early version of the literary drama which becomes peculiarly Barrett Browning's own. Its uncanny confusion of the sources of literal and creative power, of domination and inspiration, makes it the first of many poems in which she both acknowledges and repudiates the heritage of her fathers—her real father and her Romantic 'grandfathers'. It is impossible to separate the poem's intriguingly private and autobiographical elements from its public and literary ostentation.

'The Tempest' begins like a showy poetical exercise. The high-sounding, derivative rhetoric of the first lines presents a contrast between the brooding silence of Nature and the incipient violence of the storm. Within this strained register, however, there develops a gender distinction that is crucial. 'Nature', which is 'All dumb' (21), is presented as female, while the thunder is described as 'martial' (24) and male. The one is fearful, inarticulate and passive, while the other has a violent, sounding power. This contrast is then offered as a choice to the speaker. To be 'dumb' like Nature or to rage like the storm is a choice which places the poem in the tradition of the Romantic ode, and immediately turns the narrator into a would-be poet. 'Writing poetry',

Margaret Homans suggests, 'would seem to require of the writer everything that Mother Nature is not.'[28] The speaker of 'The Tempest' duly rejects the example of 'dumb' Nature, and invokes the Romantically expressive force of 'the martial thunder'.

The advent of the storm is then greeted in an enthusiastic and lofty poetical address:

> Was not my spirit gladden'd, as with wine,
> To hear the iron rain, and view the mark
> Of battle on the banner of the clouds?
> Did I not hearken for the battle-cry,
> And rush along the bowing woods to meet
> The riding Tempest—skyey cataracts
> Hissing around him with rebellion vain?
> Yea! and I lifted up my glorying voice
> In an 'All hail;' when, wildly resonant,
>   . . . the thunder cried . . .
> (37–45, 48)

This embarrassment of Romantic voices at the climax of the poem betrays the creative anxiety that lies behind its composition. The thunder does not intimidate, but inspires speech equal to its own. Like Shelley, in the 'Ode to the West Wind', this speaker goes out to meet and match the power of the elements. 'Yea! and I lifted up my glorying voice' is an ambitious attempt to rival the earlier poet's sublime inspiration. That Elizabeth Barrett's is all a storm of words might be excused by her relative youth and immaturity. Nonetheless, the engagingly derivative poeticisms in which she confidently relates this alternative story of the storm are themselves a witness to the element of creative competition in the poem. It was, after all, as she admitted many years later, precisely her fear of thunder which threatened to undermine her high 'pretension to poetry'.

The elevated address ' "All hail" ' mimics the moment of inspiration in the Romantic ode, when collaboration with some external power proves inner imaginative potential. The rhetoric of this passage rides exuberantly on the *idea* of such a collaboration. However, the interest of 'The Tempest' lies not so much in its cheerful appropriation of Romantic voices to proclaim its success, as in the way that its brave energy fails. Having triumphantly asserted the right to speak with a voice of 'thunder', the narrator does not experience the inner ebbing of energy which afflicts Shelley, but a starkly literal confrontation:

> All hail unto the lightning! hurriedly
> His lurid arms are glaring through the air,
> Making the face of heav'n to show like hell!
> Let him go breathe his sulphur stench about,
> And, pale with death's own mission, lord the storm!
> Again the gleam—the glare: I turn'd to hail
> Death's mission: at my feet there lay the dead!
> The dead—the dead lay there!
>
> (52–9)

There is a hint of moral accountability here, which is unlike anything that has gone before. The Wordsworthian 'gleam' does not turn to sad vanishings, but to a destructive 'glare', the effect of which is mercilessly literal: 'The dead—the dead lay there!'

In one sense, this is just queasily melodramatic. But in another sense, the catastrophe follows a sinister logic which cannot easily be dispelled. The consequences of daring to dissociate oneself from Nature and share the power of the storm, it seems, are death. Such heavy consequences necessarily comment on the magnitude of the act of speaking in this poem. 'Mother Nature is hardly powerless', writes Margaret Homans, 'but, enormous as her powers are, they are not the ones that her daughters want if they are to become poets.'[29] The sheer weight of the penalty that comes of speaking betrays the sex of the anonymous narrator: 'at my feet there lay the dead!' Just as she turns to hail the lightning, the *furor poeticus* of her Romantic predecessors, this speaker finds that the human consequences are laid at her feet. The storm of creativity, for Elizabeth Barrett, kills.

The melodramatic crisis of the poem clearly derives from a subtle association of two kinds of power in the poet's consciousness: the power to speak and the power to destroy. Her own youthful 'anxiety of authorship'[30] is one which recognises a strangely literal threat in the desire for creative power. The reason why Elizabeth Barrett's early attempt at the grand style of Romanticism ends in this human disaster is to be found in the unspoken fact that, for all its rhetorical derivativeness, the speaker of this poem is still a woman. This woman's 'pretension to poetry' has to overcome certain internal and external obstacles, which the poem then strangely and frighteningly realises.

The power of speech, however, does not bring down some random victim; it brings down one who is intimately known to the speaker:

> Albeit such darkness brooded all around,
> I had dread knowledge that the open eyes
> Of that dead man were glaring up to mine,
> With their unwinking, unexpressive stare;
> And mine I could not shut nor turn away.
> The man was my familiar.
>
> (85–90)

The significance of this movement from a public drama of literary ambition to a private drama of intimate emotional recognition is supplied by the suppressed idea of the father. While the thunder in one sense suggests the voices of the Romantic poets, with whom Elizabeth Barrett would compete, it is also, confusingly, the sign of one particular male presence, with whom it is dangerous and unnatural to compete: 'Only one person holds the thunder.' The new and tortured logic of this would-be Romantic poem links the poetic ambition to speak with a private drama in which the heart cannot afford to rival, in power, the object of its *tenderest and holiest affection* (Dedication to *Poems*, 1844).

'The Tempest' thus enacts the female poet's struggle to speak with a power that is not naturally her own. She refuses to be like Mother Nature, 'All dumb'. Instead, she chooses to share the thunder of the fathers: the father god, the father poets, and also, the father himself—the 'familiar'. However, to win this struggle for speech is to know, at the very moment of triumph, the cost too dear. It is this 'dread knowledge' which the poem betrays. The speaker, in the end, is shown to have harboured a death-wish towards her victim in the very act of stealing the thunder for her speech. The idea of her guilt then comes brilliantly and nightmarishly true in the figure of the dead man at her feet. Such guilt, the poem tells, is the inevitable concomitant, for the female poet, of desiring to *say* so much.

In 'The Tempest' the threat to the power of the father comes not from any rival lover, as it does in the ballads, but from poetry. Yet the drama of influence which it expresses is similarly triangular. At about the same time that she wrote 'The Tempest' Elizabeth Barrett also composed a poem which she, fortunately, never published, called 'Leila: A Tale'. It tells the story of a girl, Leila, who falls in love with a dying minstrel boy. His last request to her, before his death, is that she should use her influence to free his imprisoned father. She does so; but the shocking and unexpected outcome of this generous deed is that the boy's father acts out some ancient vow of revenge against Leila's own father, and kills him. Curiously, however, the guilt remains entirely the daughter's: 'For still her wandering lips distracted say/ "He died—I murdered him" ' (p.111).[31]

The emotional logic of the poem is clear. By desiring a rival love, Leila has betrayed her father. But there is another implication to the story. By desiring a minstrel boy, Leila reveals a wish for something else which subtly threatens her father: a wish for the boy's art of song. Behind the unconvincing melancholy tale of misplaced honour, there is an undercurrent message of literary betrayal which 'The Tempest' then develops and exaggerates.

In both poems, the father is killed by some subtle volition in the daughter who has pretensions to art. The connection is obscure, but it recurs with the force of a conviction in Barrett Browning's work. From her earliest poems to *Aurora Leigh*, the figure of the father is imagined as dead. But the timing of his death is one which resonantly implicates the daughter. He is dead, because the daughter is no longer a child, because she desires a rival lover and, finally, because she seeks the power of speech. To be a woman and a poet is to threaten the father's power. As a result, the very condition of the poem's writing is the realisation of that threat: ' "He died—I murdered him." '

In a passage from a much later work, *Casa Guidi Windows* (1851), which was written after Elizabeth's escape to Italy, the connection between literary influence and lost paternal love is made nostalgically obvious. Barrett Browning writes:

52

Could I sing this song,
  If my dead masters had not taken heed
To help the heavens and earth to make me strong,
  As the wind ever will find out some reed
And touch it to such issues as belong
  To such a frail thing? None may grudge the Dead
Libations from full cups. Unless we choose
  To look back to the hills behind us spread,
The plains before us sadden and confuse;
  If orphaned, we are disinherited.

(Part I, 432–41)[32]

What begins as a tribute to her 'dead masters' turns into a quiet commemoration of her own father, from whom she fears to be 'orphaned' and thus 'disinherited'. Masters and father are subtly confused in the motif of inspiration: 'the wind' which will fill the 'reed' of poetry. The speaker's fear of being an orphan is in one sense confirmed in the statement that the 'full cups' of her imagination's offerings are for 'the Dead'. But it is to be 'orphaned' *even* of 'the Dead' that Barrett Browning fears. For as long as those 'Dead' are still present to her imagination, the landscape of her future will keep its gladness and its meaning. The idea of 'the Dead' protects her from being quite alone in landscapes which 'sadden and confuse'; in landscapes which have no direction and no residing spirit. If the daughter loses that sense of 'dead masters', and particularly the sense of one, the 'familiar', she will be disoriented and sad in her literary endeavours. Her imagination needs the spirits of 'the Dead' if the world is not to appear forlorn and empty. If they are absent, she is 'orphaned' in the imagination; she is left without an external source of power—a muse.

Paradoxically, however, it is this very sense of being imaginatively 'disinherited' which will give to Barrett Browning's later poetry its distinctive tone. To be fatherless, or to be without a beloved object for her poetry's 'Libations from full cups', is to be in a place which is deserted and senseless. Whereas the absence of the mother will be a cause for indifference in the child poet who can be sufficient to herself, the absence of the father will be a cause of desolation and uncertainty. It is this sense of absence, of having been both 'orphaned' and 'disinherited', which marks Barrett Browning's mature poems, and which marks especially the long, daughterly quest of *Aurora Leigh*. Here, the father comes to seem, not seductively faithful and dead, as in the ballads, but simply absent. Barrett Browning's most important and most successful poem commemorates the figure of a father whom, in the end, she knows she does not need. From this harsh disinheritance comes her woman's strength.

Chapter Three

'Ghostly mother, keep aloof':
The Daughter's Disaffiliation

In October 1828, when Elizabeth Barrett was twenty-two years old, her mother died suddenly while away from home. It seems that she had been ailing for some years. Nonetheless, her death came as a shock to the rest of the family. 'The affliction was unforeseen and unexpected by me' (*Boyd*, p.62), Elizabeth wrote to her friend and mentor, Mr Boyd. In a subsequent letter she laments the loss of her mother in passionate but self-conscious phrases: 'I never can lose again what I have lost—and I never can forget what I have lost. Her voice is still sounding in my ears—her image is in my heart—and *they* are to be loved, however unreal they may be!' These faintly mannered expressions of grief may in part be attributed to Elizabeth's emotional and literary immaturity. But it is noticeable, nevertheless, that her feelings for her father, and for that father's greater loss, find a more natural expression in these letters. 'My Father is, thank God, well and composed,' she begins, and ends this same paragraph about her mother's 'voice' and 'image' with the assertion: 'But my Father's fortitude has assisted mine. After all, *his* is the great affliction . . .' (*Boyd*, p.63).

Helen Cooper[1] has accused critics and biographers of ignoring a relationship which lacks the legendary piquancy of Elizabeth's love for her father. But the evidence for this relationship is scanty. Although shocked and saddened by her mother's death, Elizabeth was not prostrated by it as she was twelve years later by the death of her brother Edward. There is a touch of self-consciousness in her expressions of grief which suggests that the 'image' of her mother is indeed a little 'unreal'. 'Oh Mr. Boyd!' she writes, 'Are we not of the earth earthy,—and must we not cling with the strong clinging of natural affection to that which is of earth . . . ?' (*Boyd*, p.62). Her tendency to moralise her feelings in these letters makes her reminiscences of her mother sound oddly self-important.

After these first declarations of grief immediately following Mary Barrett's death, Elizabeth very rarely mentions her mother again. One exception to this rule of silence is in the *Diary* of 1830–31, where, at one point, she writes with impulsive regret of her mother's love:

> How depressed I felt yesterday evening. How I hung upon the past, as if my life as well as happiness were in it! How I thought of those words *'You will never find another person who will love you as I love you'*—And how I felt that to hear again the sound of those beloved, those ever ever beloved lips, I wd. barter all other sounds & sights—that I wd. in joy & gratitude lay down before her my tastes & feelings each & all, in sacrifice for the love, the exceeding love which I never, in truth, can find again. Have I not tried this, & know this & felt this: & do I not feel *now*, bitterly, dessolately [sic], that human love like her's [sic], I never can find again! (*Diary*, p.137)

Here the fond memory of her mother serves the young Elizabeth as a comparative measure of her dissatisfaction with the present. The idea of that mother is associated with an idyllic but irrecoverable past, which the present makes poignantly rosy.

It is tempting, however, to find in this sudden outburst of despair an underplot of unrequited love for Mr Boyd. At this time, Elizabeth was spending many hours with him, reading and translating Greek. As Elaine Showalter points out, in the nineteenth century 'intelligent women aspired to study Greek and Latin with a touching faith that such knowledge would open the world of male power and wisdom to them.'[2] Mr Boyd was a classical scholar, who not only offered the young Elizabeth a precious entry into this 'world of male power', but who had the added mystique, in her eyes, of being middle-aged, blind and married. He seemed like a Miltonic figure of wisdom and insight to the young poet who was always eager to cast herself in the role of daughter. That he was another Victorian Casaubon, fusty and mean-spirited, was a fact which she overlooked in her need for a mentor, friend and intellectual authority.

The context of this passage from Elizabeth's *Diary* suggests that the memory of her mother's perfect love is thrown up suddenly in relief to some emotional disappointment connected with Mr Boyd. There is a hint of personal pique in her world-weary expression that 'human love like her's, I never can find again!' Her large-scale moralising on loss is instigated, it is clear, by something that happened 'yesterday' to make her feel 'depressed'. The evidence of most of the rest of the *Diary* is that it was some carelessness on Mr Boyd's part to confirm Elizabeth's knowledge that 'He certainly does *not* care *much* for me! not as I care for him!' (*Diary*, p.109).

The ideal memory of her mother thus serves as a rescue from the miserable facts of her youthful infatuation. The 'past' with which she is associated is an object of unreal nostalgia, which is strong only in contrast to the emotional emptiness of the present. That the mother's love is absolutely faithful and irreplaceable is a commonplace which Elizabeth eagerly repeats, but less from conviction, one feels, than from disappointment.

Other references to her mother in Barrett Browning's letters are significantly few. Only one passage, from a letter to Robert in 1846, is more than a perfunctory and formal commemoration. Here she writes that 'we lost more in Her than She lost in life, my dear dearest mother. A sweet, gentle nature, which the thunder a little turned from its sweetness—as when it turns milk—One of those women who never can resist,—but, in submitting & bowing on themselves, make a mark, a plait, within, . . a sign of suffering. Too womanly she was—it was her only fault' (*Letters: 1845–1846*, II, 1012). The 'only fault' of her mother's character was its very sweetness, although that submissiveness to 'the thunder' of her husband turned it a little sour.

This is a sympathetic and tactful criticism, but it is one that also marks out the profound difference between mother and daughter. Elizabeth herself was never in danger of being 'Too womanly'. Self-willed, independent and hungry for that knowledge conventionally reserved for men, throughout her life she tended to repudiate womanliness as the opposite of intellectual confidence and enquiry. 'I was always of a determined and if thwarted violent disposition' ('Glimpses into My Own Life', p.122), she wrote at the age of fourteen, and added, proudly: 'My mind is naturally independant [sic] and spurns that subserviency of opinion which is generally considered necessary to feminine softness' (p.131). It is likely that this somewhat triumphant confession of her faults enjoys the difference between the yielding sweetness of her mother and her own 'violent' and resisting temperament. From an early age, the choice of being a poet entailed a rejection of 'feminine softness', and therefore subtly implicated the 'sweet, gentle' figure of that mother who was to Elizabeth, still, so many years later, 'Too womanly'.

This opposition of woman and poet, which later critics resolved to the advantage of the first, is often evident in Elizabeth's own descriptions of herself. But *she* resolves the opposition differently. In a letter to Miss Mitford she boasts, for instance, that as a child she failed singularly in 'the duties belonging to my femineity'—particularly the duties of needle and thread. The reason for this failure is candidly acknowledged: 'I was always insane about books & poems—poems of my own, I mean,—& books of everybody's else . . . and, through the whole course of my childhood, I had a steady indignation against Nature who made me a woman' (*MRM*, II, 7). That 'indignation' must have included within its range the ideal of suffering femininity represented by her mother. For all her nostalgic affection for that mother, it is clear that the young poet's literary identity was forged in opposition to any 'feminine softness', and in opposition to 'the duties' of her 'femineity'. Whether she spent her days reading Homer with her brother Edward, or translating Aeschylus with Mr Boyd, the domestic life at Hope End seems largely to have passed Elizabeth by. 'Books and dreams were what I lived in' she informed Robert, '& domestic life only seemed to buzz gently around, like the bees about the grass' (*Letters: 1845–1846*, I, 41).

Her association of 'feminine softness' with intellectual subserviency was thus strengthened by the implicit choices of her own life. She chose the world of books, which was naturally connected with the three men she adored: her father, her brother Edward and Mr Boyd, rather than the world of feminine 'duties', associated with her mother. Her language often reflects this alignment. Throughout her life, she was more inclined to praise women for their manliness than for their womanliness. She warns Robert, for instance, at the start of their correspondence: 'You will find me an honest man on the whole' (*Letters: 1845–1846*, I, 13), and elsewhere she praises a certain actress for 'the "manly soul" in her face and manners', though she insists it is 'Manly, not masculine' (*Kenyon*, II, 128). Her praise of women often re-allocates the virtues traditionally ascribed to the other sex.

This dissociation of herself from the ideal of womanliness results in a highly ambivalent attitude to mother figures in Barrett Browning's poetry. The fact that many women writers at this time 'lost their mothers in early childhood'[3] may have been the reason for the high moral responsibility attached to the principle of motherhood. Mrs Gaskell, for instance, recorded the loss of her own mother as a source of lifelong deprivation: 'I think no one but one so unfortunate as to be early motherless can enter into the craving one has after the lost mother.'[4] Her own distinctly 'motherly fiction' in part bears witness to the strength of that loss. Charlotte Brontë also satisfied in fiction, in the person of Mrs Prior in *Shirley*, for instance, the motherlessness she felt in fact when nursing Emily through her last illness. By having Mrs Prior return to nurse her daughter back to health, she poignantly alters the cruel facts of Emily's death. The social ideal of motherhood as a protection, an example and a source of moral education to the daughter, is one which prevails in the Victorian novel, in spite of the fate or failure of individual mothers. But in Elizabeth Barrett's early poetry the ideal itself can be seen to be distrusted.

The reason for this is that the figure of the mother comes to stand, not so much in a social relation to the daughter, but in the relation of muse to poet. In the mother, the daughter poet looks for a figure to spur her desire and ambition, but finds instead a figure who merely enjoins on her the principles of generosity and self-sacrifice. Such a figure thus implicitly denies the daughter's quest for self-fulfilling power. 'Too womanly she was—it was her only fault.' Womanliness is naturally the opposite of that poetic ambition which seeks an image of self-confirming power to the imagination. The daughter poet cannot afford to be like her mother and to submit and bow to 'the thunder'. She must resist it, or even rival it, herself.

Elizabeth Barrett's early poetry is especially sensitive to the threat from this ideal of womanliness. Whether that womanliness be embodied in the ghost of the mother, in the female personification of the past, or in the lady spirit of the garden, all these variations of the imagination's muse are figures to which the daughter poet is strangely antagonistic. Her dalliance with the mother muse is a dalliance not with love, as in the case of the father, but with death. This prevailing sense of deathliness in the figure of the woman is one which offers no emotional compensations for the daughter's self-denial. As a result, those early poems which contain a ghostly female presence betray an anxiety of womanliness in the speaker, and a subsequent imaginative struggle for disaffiliation, which is very different from her close and seductive conflict with the father. While she fears to lose the oppressive but inspiring authority of the father, this daughter poet is glad to repudiate the colder commands of the mother.

'The Romaunt of Margret' (1838) is an early ballad which seems to invoke a traditional figure of the 'belle dame sans merci'. Margret sits by the riverside when a fair pale lady rises up out of her own rippling shadow. It seems, therefore, that she is a figure for Margret's self. But then the lady taunts Margret with the fact that neither her brother, sister, father nor betrothed returns her love—the hint being that only the mother, who is conspicuously absent from the list, is constant. The poem recalls the words Elizabeth remembered her own mother saying: ' "*You will never find another person who will love you as I love you.*" ' Margret at first bravely answers the taunts of faithlessness. But when the lady reveals that her last hope, her lover, is in fact dead, she gives up, and like her other literary sisters of the ballad, kills herself.

The poem is only interesting because the traditional 'fair ladye' (II)[5] is not a seductress, but a mother. ' "Am I not like to thee?" ' (65) she asks threateningly. She rises up out of Margret's shadow like her double, and tempts her daughter with the knowledge that all human love is faithless by comparison with hers. While the poem suffers—as does Elizabeth Barrett's commemoration of her own mother in her *Diary*—from a kind of pique at finding the world loveless, it also reveals a new fearfulness of what the mother represents. The shadow lady, with pallid brow and fixed smile, threatens Margret with the fateful similarity between them:

> For so will sound thy voice
>   When thy face is to the wall,
> And such will be thy face, ladye,
>   When the maidens work thy pall.
> (60–3)

The features which reflect Margret's are those of death.

The shadow lady tempts her, not with a more true love than those of earth, but with a deathly fate which she desires the daughter also to inherit. Unlike the ghostly father, who calls the daughter ' "my beloved" ', the ghostly mother calls her for the more sinister and menacing reason: ' "Am I not like to thee?" '

This difference is evident in another of these ballads which plays out the daughter's choice of being a child or a woman, of being faithful to her past or to her present. In 'Bertha in the Lane' (1844), it is again not the father but the mother who is the rival for the daughter's life. Consequently, although the triangular situation is the same, the emotional atmosphere is quite different. The poem tells the story of two sisters. The elder has lost her lover to her younger sister Bertha, whom she has overheard dallying with that lover 'in the lane'. However, she acts with stoical magnanimity, and speaks to set the younger's conscience at rest. But it is wrong to regard her, therefore, as Gilbert and Gubar do, as a 'dying angel'.[6] The dramatic conflict of the poem is not between the two sisters, but between the elder sister and the ghostly presence of the mother. It is this third presence which characteristically complicates the poem's apparently banal sentiments.

The elder sister invokes her dead mother as a moral guide:

> Mother, mother, up in heaven,
>   Stand up on the jasper sea,
> And be witness I have given
>   All the gifts required of me,—
> Hope that blessed me, bliss that crowned,
> Love that left me with a wound,
> Life itself that turneth round!
>
> (36–42)[7]

63

The basis of the mother's moral authority lies in the fact that the elder sister is naturally assumed to have taken her place. 'Have I not been nigh a mother . . . ?' (29) she insists, and it is because she has acceded to this role of substitute mother that she acts with such self-denying generosity towards her younger sister. However, it is not only the lover she is expected to relinquish. She must also give, in the true spirit of motherhood, her own life for her child. Not only 'Hope' and 'Love' are required of her, but also 'Life itself that turneth round!' This is not a supererogatory sentimental addition to the story; it is of the very essence of the elder sister's new role. To give 'All the gifts required of me' is to accept the harsh prerogative and fate of the mother 'up in heaven'. It is not sisterly generosity which provides the moral of the tale, but motherly duty.

This is the reason why the poem is not just a sentimental condoning of womanly self-sacrifice. The presence of the ghostly mother is an interpolation which the story does not need, and which, by introducing an element of compulsion, distorts and spoils the message of the tale. Against this compulsion the language subtly protests. The elder sister gives 'All the gifts *required*' of her, and the true nature of that requirement is then shown in the apparition of the mother herself:

> Mother, mother, thou art kind,
>   Thou art standing in the room,
> In a molten glory shrined
>   That rays off into the gloom!
> But thy smile is bright and bleak
> Like cold waves—I cannot speak,
> I sob in it, and grow weak.
>
> (43–9)

In spite of the saintly light in which she is 'shrined', like some last Madonna, the figure of the mother seems cold and cruel. She appears in the guise of a frozen effigy to the daughter's imagination. The prize which awaits the woman who is prepared to be a mother too, and give up life for her surrogate daughter, is to become a saint in 'molten glory'. But the bleak, senseless piety of the mother's 'smile', unlike the temptations of the father's smile, merely appals the daughter. It is cold, inhuman and exacting.

At this point, the elder sister rejects the mother's fate which awaits her:

> Ghostly mother, keep aloof
> One hour longer from my soul,
> For I still am thinking of
> Earth's warm-beating joy and dole!
>
> (50–3)

What she sees in the 'Ghostly mother' is merely the contradiction of her own desire to live and love. But unlike the similar contradiction offered by the father, there is no emotional compensation here. The freezing, saintly image of the mother requires her daughter's similar self-renunciation, and smiles eternally for her death. The suicidal impulse of the ending has no emotional logic to it, but merely reinforces the idea of maternal duty. This particular elder daughter perceives too clearly that the saintly ideal of motherhood is an ideal that kills.

In these ballads, the figure of the ghostly mother is a figure of self-renunciation and of despair. She does not entice the daughter with better love, but compels her with rigid moral requirements. The daughter must renounce life in order to fulfil the role allotted to her: the role of womanly self-sacrifice. However, what is apparent in these poems is the daughter's abhorrence of that role of the death which she inherits. The emotional emphasis in them is one which forcefully rejects the fate and the moral authority of the mother, whose claim to the life of the daughter is not based on love but on the duties of their shared womanliness.

However, in other early poems Elizabeth Barrett expresses her imagination's distrust of the figure of the mother more subtly. In these, the mother becomes a haunting spirit of the place, a *genius loci*, and in particular a spirit of the garden. Such a presence has strong Wordsworthian overtones, as in the early poem called 'The Past' (1826), where she is imagined as one who will 'speak to me in places lone' (27).[8] In her papers on poetry for the *Athenaeum* Elizabeth Barrett defines the beginnings of Romanticism as the dawn-time of Mother Nature: 'Nature, the true mother, cried afar off to her children.' That Nature is a mothering presence has a long tradition which she unquestioningly accepts, and of which she takes Wordsworth to be the greatest exponent. It is he who with 'filial familiarity' and 'trustfully as child before mother'[9] looks to Nature as his inspiration. This strong association is one which the daughter poet inherits and for which there is no convincing substitute. Nature is a mothering, not a fathering, muse.

Nonetheless, her unease becomes evident in those poems which take the form of a quest for the spirit of Nature. Such a spirit is traditionally female, and she is also traditionally a muse to inspire poems in the quester. However, there is a curious literalness in Elizabeth Barrett's perception of that spirit, and it betrays her essentially female anxieties of authorship. The place where such a spirit resides is in the lost garden of childhood. The many poems about a garden haunted by the spirit of a woman bear witness to the weight of an inherited tradition of the *genius loci* as female, but they also draw on a more specific and biographical association. Two years after her own mother's death, Elizabeth wrote in her *Diary* of 1830 that 'B & I went out to walk; & into the garden, for the first time since that loss which must be a loss for ever. I mean, Bummy's first time—not mine. *I* have been there very often' (*Diary*, p.198). Clearly this garden was one of Mrs Barrett's haunts, and the memory of her is strong in Elizabeth's consciousness as she walks there with her aunt. However, *she* has been to this secret garden 'very often' before, and the faint note of bravura suggests that it is a strong imaginative draw on the young poet. Yet in two poems which take the form of a literary quest for the spirit of the garden, the female presence which it harbours is an object of strange distrust and disaffection. If, as Geoffrey Hartman writes in 'Romantic Poetry and the *Genius Loci*', the poet quests for the spirit of the place as a figure for 'his own identity',[10] then the daughter poet who quests for the female spirit of the place risks finding her identity, not in the context of courtship and sexual union, in a 'ceremonial merging',[11] but in relation to the dead mother. Such a figure does not nourish but rather denies the self-identity which the daughter seeks. The powers of 'Mother Nature', as Homans writes, 'are not the ones that her daughters want if they are to become poets.'[12]

'The Deserted Garden' (1838) tells of a secret garden, forgotten by all except a solitary child who plays there. The poem is spoken by the adult poet, however, who remembers the garden with regret as the place of her own lost childhood's passion. A Wordsworthian philosophy of compensation, that 'We draw the moral afterward,/We feel the gladness then' (55–6),[13] seems to lie at the heart of the poem's message. However, there is another reason for the poet's self-division into adult and child. The child shows a cheerful indifference to the haunting spirits of the place—an indifference which the adult speaker envies and, in the end, approves.

The speaker remembers the white roses in the garden, but her adult imagination then summons to mind the human presence which the roses seem to recall:

> Some lady, stately overmuch,
> Here moving with a silken noise,
> Has blushed beside them at the voice
>   That likened her to such.
>
> And these, to make a diadem,
> She often may have plucked and twined,
> Half-smiling as it came to mind
>   That few would look at *them*.
>
> (29–36)

This mysterious first inhabitant of the garden moves as lightly as the sound of leaves and is as white as the white roses. She is in some sense the humanised genius of the place. However, she is not like Shelley's lady of the garden in 'The Sensitive Plant', for instance, because she is too regal and narcissistic. She despoils the roses and she intrudes her human consciousness in the place. Above all, she is unlike the Romantic *genius loci* because she is not a figure for something that the poet desires to find. Quite the contrary. Elizabeth Barrett makes it plain that the white lady is waiting for someone else—for another 'voice' to compare her with the roses. For that other quester, who is adult and male, the beautiful self-conscious white lady easily out-shines white roses and is, therefore, the natural goal of his journey to the garden.

But for this speaker the lady is not an object of admiration:

> Oh, little thought that lady proud,
> A child would watch her fair white rose,
> When buried lay her whiter brows,
> And silk was changed for shroud!
> (37–40)

There is an almost punishing satisfaction in this last comparison of the lady with the roses. Her brows are now only 'whiter' for being dead, and the child, with her curious child's indifference to love and ladies, is glad to find *only* roses. 'How should I know but roses might/Lead lives as glad as mine?' (63–4) she asserts. Instead of courting the lady of the garden as the desirable spirit of the place to answer the imagination's quest, both speaker and child disown her. She is no beloved muse with whom to dally. For the speaker she is too 'proud' and self-conscious—'stately overmuch'. To the child she is irrelevant, and the garden harbours nothing but flowers and birds. The real object of the speaker's poetic quest is not the seductive ghostly woman, but the literal-minded and self-sufficient child, who has no concern for the dead: 'It did not move my grief to see/ The trace of human step departed' (49–50).

This is a quest poem which leads to disenchantment rather than to an encounter. It imagines a lovers' meeting in the garden, but such a meeting is for others. Meanwhile, the child poet herself needs no ghostly presences or secret spirits, and in their very absence makes her imagination's playtime. The white lady represents the threat of womanliness, which is strongly connected, once again, with death. So the threat is repudiated, and instead the garden is found to be indeed 'deserted'. The female genius of the place is absent, and it is from that absence that the Victorian daughter's poetic quest proceeds. She portrays herself, not as the lover in search of a 'fair ladye', but as the child who is content to find the place empty. This sense of desertion enforces a sense of being, not only without the mother, but also without a muse. The child's imagination is unhaunted and therefore 'orphaned'.

A second poem about a garden, 'The Lost Bower' (1844), is a long, domesticated quest romance, which often echoes Wordsworth's 'Nutting'. But whereas Wordsworth's quester is a boy poet who finds a sister 'spirit in the woods' (56),[14] Elizabeth Barrett's is a female quester, whose object is uncertain. The poem tells of the child's discovery of a secret, natural bower, which it is clear from the start represents the place of poetry. A long literary tradition of finding a lady in the woods supports this child's quest:

> And the poets wander, said I,
> Over places all as rude:
> Bold Rinaldo's lovely lady
> Sat to meet him in a wood:
> Rosalinda, like a fountain, laughed out pure with solitude.

> And if Chaucer had not travelled
> Through a forest by a well,
> He had never dreamt nor marvelled
> At those ladies fair and fell
> Who lived smiling without loving in their island-citadel.
>
> (66–75)[15]

The child eagerly seeks to follow in this tradition. She is drawn to the woods in the hope of finding what the poets of old found there: a 'lovely lady'. It was in such

places that the beloved and inspiring muse of poetry was
to be met.

Thus the child uses the thought of her past masters,
her revered 'grandfathers', to help her get into the bower
of poetry:

> Thus I thought of the old singers
> And took courage from their song,
> Till my little struggling fingers
> Tore asunder gyve and thong
> Of the brambles which entrapped me, and the barrier
> branches strong.
>
> (76–80)

Clearly, the whole enterprise of getting into the bower is
a figure for her creativity. This child poet utilises the
influence of 'the old singers' to help her work her way
through the obstructing difficulties of her craft. She
persists, and then with inspirational suddenness, that is
touchingly indebted to her favourite old singer,
Wordsworth, she gains an entry to the bower: 'I was
gladdened unaware' (85). The place, when she enters it,
is spacious and hospitable, and is more like a garden than
a wood. In one sense, she has found her way back to an
Eden beyond nature, which is controlled and curbed
without toil. In another sense, her laborious craft has
suddenly released its unexpected inspiration. The bower
is the primal garden, and it is also the inspirational
reward for her toil. This rather delicate and witty
description of the growth of a poet's mind plays lightly
between ordinary narrative and quest allegory.

Once inside the bower, however, the child again
thinks that she might find, like 'the old singers' before
her, some 'spirit in the woods', a *genius loci*—of course, a
lady:

> Oh, a lady might have come there,
> Hooded fairly like her hawk,
> With a book or lute in summer,
> And a hope of sweeter talk,—
> Listening less to her own music than for footsteps
>   on the walk!
>
> (106–10)

This is one in a long line of damsels encountered in wood or forest by the anxiously wandering poet. Such a lady promises to inspire a dream of love. However, like the lady of 'The Deserted Garden', this one too is looking away. She is listening, it is clear, for another's 'footsteps on the walk'. The child poet is not the lover she expects, and for whom she might read or play. Such a 'lady' belongs to someone else's imagination: to Chaucer's or Ariosto's.

As a result, the child's path begins to digress from that marked out by her past masters. She quests for a different spirit of the place:

> Down to floor and up to ceiling
> Quick I turned my childish face,
> With an innocent appealing
> For the secret of the place
> To the trees, which surely knew it in partaking of the
>   grace.
>
> (146–50)

Having failed to find a dream lady, she looks for some other hidden 'secret of the place' to marry with her imagination's needs, and confirm her identity as a poetic quester. She wonders if there might be other sources of enchantment: 'Nature' (153) or some 'Dryad' (162) or even 'fairies' (166).

Then, even as she wonders, the place releases its 'secret':

> So, young muser, I sat listening
> To my fancy's wildest word:
> On a sudden, through the glistening .
> Leaves around, a little stirred,
> Came a sound, a sense of music which was rather felt
> than heard.
>
> (171–5)

A little disappointingly, at first, the secret seems to be the music of her Romantic predecessors, which is 'rather felt than heard'. Such music has been felt very often before. However, this is not the end of her quest. The music creates a bower within the bower, and within it there is a diminutive presence:

> Softly, finely, it inwound me;
> From the world it shut me in,—
> Like a fountain, falling round me,
> Which with silver waters thin
> Clips a little water Naiad sitting smilingly within.
>
> (176–80)

The 'secret of the place' is here. The *genius loci* is this 'little water Naiad' embowered in the fountain of music. She is, of course, a figure for the child poet herself. The end of the daughter's quest is to find herself mirrored in the bower of her own music. This 'young muser' finds, mischievously, that she is indeed her own muse, and that the object of her quest is a mirror-image; 'sitting smilingly', as if at the joke.

Once again, the young Elizabeth Barrett sets out on a traditional quest but finds a different goal. There is no seductive lady, no enchantress, no maddening dream of love. Instead, there is only herself in a bower full of ordinary leaves and flowers. Yet, out of these comes enchanting music, and a sense of self that is doubly strong. 'Henceforth, I will be the fairy/ Of this bower' (241–2), she declares, thus affirming what the poem has

73

already told. This new 'young muser', who followed so keenly in the path of her masters, finds in the end that the bower of poetry is deserted, like the garden, and that only her own reflection can serve as a muse.

'The Lost Bower' is a delightful rewriting of the quest romance from the point of view of the daughter poet. She journeys through the dark woods and forests of poetry, but finds all the lovely ladies either dead or looking away, and all the old enchantments fled. In this bare and ordinary landscape, from which ghosts and spirits have been banished, she marries instead with her own reflection. Subject and object mirror each other perfectly in the poem's fluid imagery of bower–music–water, which is the imagery of its own composition. Simply by writing, the daughter poet saves and reconstitutes the bower of poetry around the self-sufficient image of 'a little water Naiad sitting smilingly within'. She is her own genius of the place.

These early poems which invoke the authority of the mother or the inspiration of the lovely lady all betray the daughter poet's distrust and disaffiliation. The mother is a cold and deathly figure, who tempts the daughter to give her life for womanly duty rather than to save it for poetry. The lady muse simply expects someone else to court her. The daughter's poetic identity is thus denied by both: by the moral requirements of the one and by the sexual indifference of the other.

As a result, the quest for her poetry's inspiration leads to a place which is empty of presences. Both the bower and the garden are deserted, not only in the sense of being lost to the adult poet, but in the sense of being without the spirits of enchantment. Such a place suggests, on the one hand, the Victorian poet's loss of poetic hauntings. But, on the other hand, it also suggests the daughter poet's ambition to be different. If the

Romantic spirits of the place have been lost and dispersed, this is also in part because the daughter poet rejects them. The landscapes of Barrett Browning's mature poems will bear this imprint of something that is absent, and which must be absent if she is to survive the strong authority not only of 'the grandfathers', but also of the powerful figures of her own family.

Chapter Four

'I cannot write of these things': The Woman's Silence

When Elizabeth was fourteen, her brother Edward, known affectionately as Bro, was sent away to school. With only a year between them in age, Elizabeth and Bro had long been inseparable companions and literary confederates. After his departure for school, Elizabeth wrote: 'If I ever loved any human being I love this dear Brother . . the Partner of my pleasures of my literary toils. My attachment to him is literally devoted!' and added, magnanimously: 'If to save him from anxiety from mental vexation any effort of mine could suffice Heaven knows my heart that I would unhesitatingly buy his happiness with my own misery!' ('Glimpses into My Own Life', p.129). School parted them, as it did Marian Evans from her beloved brother, Isaac. It was at about this time that Elizabeth suffered an injury to her spine, and Betty Miller suggests that the long invalidism which followed was in part a psychological reaction to Bro's departure.[1] However, her further suggestion that the relationship between brother and sister was a violent and quarrelsome one, based on physical and intellectual rivalry,[2] is not supported by Elizabeth's own comments. She wrote: 'my dearest Bro tho my constant companion and a beloved participator in all my pleasures never allowed the rage for power to injure the endearing sweetness of his temper' ('Glimpses into My Own Life', p.123). Many years later she stressed the fact, to Miss Mitford, that there was 'no harsh word, no unkind look—never from my babyhood till I stood alone' (*MRM*, I, 226). To Robert, she asserted that he was 'kindest & noblest & dearest to *me*, beyond comparison' (*Letters: 1845-1846*, I, 170).

That these are not just retrospectively rosy memories is supported by the facts of Bro's own short life. That 'rage for power' in the nursery seems never to have developed in him, as it did in his sister, into literary ambition. His adult occupation remains unknown;[3] while the ease and readiness with which he agreed to accompany and stay with Elizabeth in Torquay for some two years suggests that his commitments were not very pressing. Furthermore, there seems to have been a trait of listlessness in his character, which Elizabeth herself hints at when she writes that he had 'high talents—only not distinguished among men, because the heart was too tender for energy—Only God who is love, knew how tender to *me*' (*MRM*, I, 306). This tells a different story from Miller's. It suggests that the very strength of the relationship between Elizabeth and Bro came from an absence of rivalry that was due, probably not to Elizabeth's own violent and wilful disposition, but to the easy tenderness and natural supportiveness of her brother. Elizabeth's later memories of Bro's sweetness, kindness and tenderness find a kind of fit corroboration in the very obscurity of evidence about his life.

However, he was for many years her literary

companion and arbiter. Although Elizabeth wrote her poems ultimately to gain the approving smile of her father, it seems that it was really Bro whom she could trust to appreciate and judge them. It was his literary perceptiveness which she remembered later, when she told Miss Mitford that 'there is no one close to me always, to whom I can say "Is this which I have written, good? Is it worth anything?" and, be sure of the just answer' (*MRM*, I, 226). Her father's smile was her high reward, but her brother's judgement was alone trustworthy.

Two early poems portray this brother in a role very similar to that of Elizabeth's father. He is a moral guide and the beloved object of her literary addresses. In 'A True Dream', which was never published, the dreamer conjures up three serpents—deadly but fascinating creatures—which her brother tries to exorcise for her:

> Outspake that pitying brother of mine—
> 'Now nay, my sister, nay,
> I will pour on them oil of vitriol,
> And burn their lives away.'[4]

He too, like her father, is a moral rescue from the brilliant, horrifying figments of her dreams. But there is a hint of regret in her observation of his saving actions: 'the serpents writhed in agony/Beneath my dreaming eyes.' In the end, the poem tells, this brother cannot save her from the power of the serpents, which fantastically metamorphose into a deathly figure who pursues and claims her. The 'pitying brother' cannot control her possession by the forces of her dreams. 'Verses to My Brother' (1826), on the other hand, is simply a declaration of affection and of nostalgia for a childhood spent reading and writing together:

My Brother! dearest, kindest as thou art!
How can these lips my heart's affection prove?
I could not speak the words, if words could speak my love.
(8–10)[5]

This kindly, protective figure was to be lost to Elizabeth's imagination when she was thirty-four, and the epigraph from *Lycidas* at the start of this poem seems like a terrible, careless portent of that loss.

On 11 July 1840, Bro went sailing with some friends. Elizabeth had been sent to Torquay two years earlier to convalesce, and had insisted, against her father's will, that her favourite brother should not return to London but should remain with her. She remembered her father's moral opposition to her demand with the lacerating bitterness of hindsight: '"he considered it to be *very wrong in me to enact such a thing.*"' The sheer magnitude of that wrong was to be impressed upon her imagination for the rest of her life. On that fatal day, Bro did not return. 'For three days we waited—& I hoped while I could—oh—that awful agony of three days! And the sun shone as it shines to-day, & there was no more wind than now; and the sea under the windows was like this paper for smoothness' (*Letters: 1845–1846*, I, 170), she told Robert. It was the senseless treachery of that sea which could not be erased from her memory, and was to seem like the sign of her guilt almost to the end of her life. After those three days, Elizabeth 'lay for weeks & months half conscious, half unconscious, with a wandering mind'. Above all, she was not 'able to shed then one tear' (*Letters: 1845–1846*, I, 171).

To chart the rare expressions of grief in Barrett Browning's letters is to find how heavy a burden of feeling the idea of silence carries. 'I cannot write of these things' is a phrase which comes round with heartfelt, if dull, repetitiveness. Bro, she tells, was 'the only one of my family who . . well, but I cannot write of these things' (*Letters: 1845–1846*, I, 170), and she then abruptly commands Robert never to raise the subject again: 'I have never said so much to a living being—I never *could* speak or write of it' (I, 171). Twenty years after the death of Bro, the death of her sister Henrietta in 1860 pitched Elizabeth back into the same inarticulateness, which is heavy with the sound of all her old griefs: 'My dear dear friend it has not been easy for me to write—I never can write or speak. I am congealed by grief always, & the tears which come to nearly everybody will not come to me' (*Ogilvy*, p. 167). Each new death came as a reminder of one for which there could never be grief and silence enough in Barrett Browning's poetically productive life.

It is strange that, even after the enormous compensations of her marriage, Elizabeth was still liable to succumb to the despair of the past. She wrote in the summer of 1851, at the height of her happiness, of 'only one event in my life which never loses its bitterness; which comes back on me like a retreating wave, going and coming again, which was and *is my grief—I never had but one brother who loved and comprehended me*' (*Kenyon*, II, 14). That event, like the loss of Hallam for Tennyson, was to be a lifelong draw on her imagination. It drew her, however, not into more poetry, but into dumbness. Grief could never nourish in her so long and indefatigable a poem as *In Memoriam*, for that would have seemed a travesty of her true feelings. Nonetheless, when *In Memoriam* was published, she wrote about it with the perspicuity of her own similar grief. 'The monotony is a part of the position—the sea is montononous, & so is lasting grief . . . Who that has suffered, has not felt wave after wave break dully against one rock' (*MRM*, III, 318), she insisted to Miss Mitford. Ten years after the event, her imagination's ear could still hear the sound of waves breaking on the shore at Torquay.

However, while Tennyson wrote his long elegy to anaesthetise grief, to allay it, to order it and, finally, to share it, Elizabeth Barrett could never forgive herself enough to seek such consolation. That she was in some subtle, superstitious way responsible for Bro's death was an idea that she could not rationalise. The calm sea, the safe bay, the summer's day, all returned to mock her with the absurd deliberateness of the event. This guilt and superstition of evil in herself resulted in a lifelong grief for Bro which was not only inconsolable, but also imaginatively unredeemable. 'I cannot write of these things—I cannot write or speak—I never have spoken—not one word—not to Papa—never named that name anymore' (*MRM*, I, 306), she protested vehemently to Miss Mitford. Those few fine poems she did in fact write about grief and loss bear witness to the pressure of that absent name. The special silence of the grieving sonnets comes from this strong sense of namelessness at their heart.

There has been a long tradition in western literature of finding in the principle of silence the truest form of speech: a speech of the heart, for instance, which writing damagingly makes public; or a speech of God's, which impresses like inspiration. As George Steiner has shown, 'the motif of the necessary limitations of the human word is a frequent one', and he lists 'light, music, and silence'[6] as the most common resonances beyond the written word in English poetry. There has also been, in recent feminist criticism, a desire to claim silences as a peculiarly female right—to claim them as a sign of oppression which can be turned into protest. Xavière Gauthier writes, among many others, that it is especially the task of women's writing to *make audible* that which agitates within us, suffers silently in the *holes of discourse*'.[7]

By claiming silences, verbally, women might challenge male discourse without simply imitating it. By disrupting speech, women might open a passage to what speech, by its very nature, disallows. Such silences, however, are not in their essence different from the silences of religious or Romantic literature, for instance. They are different only in their *reasons* for making felt the pressure of an alternative discourse in writing.

For Elizabeth Barrett, the silence of her grief makes itself audible, not in any strategic verbal disruption, but in a sense of imaginative absence. The few grieving sonnets published in 1844 do not express a mystical aspiration towards a more authentic, ineffable speech of the heart, nor do they mime in verbal collapse the stops and starts of sorrow. Their silence is not part of the linguistic structure of the poem, but is, instead, its opposite. Such silence is a despair of naming: 'I never have spoken—not one word—not to Papa—never named that name anymore.' That refusal to *name* the object of her grief is a silence upon which the words of these sonnets skate thinly. In that silence is preserved the figure of Bro.

Unlike the name of the father, then, and the figure of the mother, the name and figure of Bro are suppressed in these poems. They do not steady themselves against a presence which authorises their writing. Instead, that presence is lacking, and the poems constantly deny the validity of their writing. Their words remain at a long distance from that deep dumbness which most truly expresses the speaker's feelings. Caught between the truth of speechlessness and the compulsion to speak of the hardest things, Elizabeth Barrett finds words which say just enough to make her despair of speaking *heard*. It is perhaps a characteristic of the female imagination to desire that silence which is an abdication of all poetic power, rather than a culmination of it. This poet refuses to invoke any name or any figure to support the truth of her writing. In these sonnets, Bro is never named or hailed or encountered by the living speaker, whose gift of speech seems like a far and irrelevant sound compared to his silence. Somehow, these poems are too honest to imagine that their muse is anything except simply dead.

'I *know* that I would have died ten times over for *him*' (*Letters: 1845–1846*, I, 171), Elizabeth insisted to Robert. But her fate was the harder one of living on, and of being able to write poems still. The sense of shame at her own power to write but not to die is a strong negative impulse behind these elegies. Many years later, when Henrietta was dying of cancer and Elizabeth could not travel to England to nurse her, she wrote that it was her cruel fate 'to have only power at the end of my pen, and for the help of people I don't care for' (*Kenyon*, II, 405–6). The few poems she wrote about the death of Bro seem to be inspired, not by the effort of expressing grief, but by the effort of being dumb, somehow, against the 'power' of her own 'pen'. It is that dumbness which these most reluctant elegies throw into relief.

> Thank God, bless God, all ye who suffer not
> More grief than ye can weep for. That is well—
> That is light grieving! lighter, none befell
> Since Adam forfeited the primal lot.
> Tears! what are tears? The babe weeps in its cot,
> The mother singing; at her marriage-bell
> The bride weeps, and before the oracle
> Of high-faned hills the poet has forgot
> Such moisture on his cheeks. Thank God for grace,
> Ye who weep only! If, as some have done,
> Ye grope tear-blinded in a desert place
> And touch but tombs,—look up! those tears will run
> Soon in long rivers down the lifted face,

And leave the vision clear for stars and sun.
('Tears')[8]

In spite of the rigorous formal requirements of the Petrarchan sonnet, the register of these poems is unexpectedly relaxed. Their pace is that of the speaking voice, which thus gives an impression of intimacy and ease. The impression is false, however, because far from being personal confidences, these are considered, philosophical poems about the nature of grief, addressed to some generalised reader from the presumed vantage-point of grief that has been overcome. The tone of this sonnet is one of bitterly learned resignation: 'Thank God, bless God, all ye who suffer not/More grief than ye can weep for.' The whole poem then offers its message of consolation to those who weep: babies, mothers, brides, and poets too, who can weep in admiration of high hills. These, the sonnet tells, are all the lucky descendants of Adam, who grieved for Eden, but would be divinely consoled for the loss.

This remedy of tears then carries with it the conviction of an imaginative revelation. Consolation comes like visionary insight at the end of the poem:

> look up! those tears will run
> Soon in long rivers down the lifted face,
> And leave the vision clear for stars and sun.

The poem puts its message to effect. These fine, apocalyptic last lines express a sudden inspiration of comfort, which links the effort of poetry with the end of grief. This is the link that will be made so powerfully in section *XCV* of *In Memoriam*. The poet's vision will be a vision which restores the dead. In this sonnet, such a 'vision' will restore the natural consolation of 'stars and sun', in a new, inspired clarity of sight.

However, the rhetorical force of these last lines is undercut by something else in the poem: 'Thank God for grace,/Ye who weep only!' Its promise of hope and its triumphant 'vision' are for those 'who weep only'; they are not for those others—unmentioned but implied—who cannot weep. 'I am congealed by grief always, & the tears which come to nearly everybody will not come to me,' Barrett Browning wrote. The whole sonnet hides an alternative message, which is, that those who cannot weep cannot be consoled. Those are exempt even from Adam's cure. For those benighted ones, the fine, uplifting vision at the end is pointless, and the rewarding metaphor of new sight simply does not work. Because they are not 'tear-blinded', they see their way quite clearly in that 'desert place' full of 'tombs', and need no new 'stars and sun' for compensation. The person who speaks and writes this sonnet of visionary hope remains bleakly unmoved by the consolation she works out.

What the poem finely but not quite inaudibly leaves in silence is that other message of despair. The speaker is calm and philosophical, and does not pretend to confide any personal feeling. She tells of Christian redemption and of visionary revelation. But neither of these is for the ones who cannot weep. The very imaginative success of the poem remains ineffective, and at a long distance from the speaker who is speaking so calmly only because she has no hope—of weeping. Thus the poem is an exercise in consolation, which shuts out, beyond the margins of its verbal comforts, a grief which cannot be caught up into poetry. Such grief contradicts everything the poem offers. The tearless go on walking among 'tombs' on the desert plain, with terrible, changeless clarity of sight. These do not need sublime views of the skies.

What Elizabeth Barrett relegates to silence in these

poems is something which denies and shames their writing. The unnamed object of her grief creates a verbal absence in the poem, against which all its writing rings hollow. True grief is inconsolable because the dead cannot be named, invoked and recovered in the mourner's imagination. Visions are for others, and so are poems.

This is the uncompromising message also of the sonnet called 'Grief':

> I tell you, hopeless grief is passionless;
> That only men incredulous of despair,
> Half-taught in anguish, through the midnight air
> Beat upward to God's throne in loud access
> Of shrieking and reproach. Full desertness,
> In souls as countries, lieth silent-bare
> Under the blanching, vertical eye-glare
> Of the absolute Heavens. Deep-hearted man, express
> Grief for thy Dead in silence like to death—
> Most like a monumental statue set
> In everlasting watch and moveless woe
> Till itself crumble to the dust beneath.
> Touch it; the marble eyelids are not wet:
> If it could weep, it could arise and go.
>
> ('Grief')[9]

Grief, she declares, is not an overflowing of the heart's true feelings; it is still and 'passionless'. It makes no sound and has no movements. Those who go noisily seeking the consolation of God are 'incredulous' of the real creed of despair. These other true believers stay still and silent among the tombs of the desert, matching their grief to the state of the 'Dead'. Such grief is an unmoving, crumbling statue, like Shelley's 'Ozymandias',[10] which has no point except to commemorate its own transience:

Most like a monumental statue set
In everlasting watch and moveless woe
Till itself crumble to the dust beneath.

This powerful figure of dumbness is like the poem's negative. Only by being cold, blind and dumb as a stone will the mourner be able to *express* grief; only by being fixed and nameless will this 'monumental statue' be an authentic figure for the dead. Silent, still and crumbling, it is a figure of what can never be saved for poetry, and all poetry's temptations to hope: 'Touch it; the marble eyelids are not wet:/If it could weep, it could arise and go.' The lines are almost witty in their logic: 'If it could weep', it would not be a statue. In actuality, it cannot weep, move, feel or speak, and the point of a statue is proved.

Like the sonnet 'Tears', this one also refuses to transform 'hopeless grief' into imaginative exhilaration, in the way that elegiac writing for Milton, Shelley and Tennyson, for instance, brings hope through a visionary effort of belief that the dead live on. Elizabeth Barrett's are elegies which will not change the beloved lost object into an aspiration for poetry. In place of the name or figure of Bro there is an absence—something unwritten. The statue of grief is one which bears no name or inscription for posterity. It is not an epitaph, but a blank.

In these sonnets Elizabeth Barrett exposes the difference between what is written and what is real. This female elegist will not use the 'power at the end of [her] pen' to control or transform the reality of Bro's death, nor will she invoke his presence as a muse. Instead, she separates the silence that marks his name, from the poetry that speaks on. On one level, therefore, she declaims with passionate rhetoric: 'I tell you'; but on another level she remains as if absent from the poem and quite dumb: 'in silence like to death'. Between the two there is an insuperable disparity.

The sonnet called 'Substitution' is the last which enacts this self-denying discourse on silence:

> When some belovèd voice that was to you
> Both sound and sweetness, faileth suddenly,
> And silence, against which you dare not cry,
> Aches round you like a strong disease and new—
> What hope? what help? what music will undo
> That silence to your sense? Not friendship's sigh,
> Not reason's subtle count; not melody
> Of viols, nor of pipes that Faunus blew;
> Not songs of poets, nor of nightingales
> Whose hearts leap upward through the cypress-trees
> To the clear moon; nor yet the spheric laws
> Self-chanted, nor the angels' sweet 'All hails,'
> Met in the smile of God: nay, none of these.
> Speak THOU, availing Christ!—and fill this pause.
>
> ('Substitution')"

All this poem's speeches serve only to point up that silence which takes the place of the 'belovèd voice'. The speaker casts about for sounds: for the 'sigh' of a friend, for the 'count' of reason, for music and poetry. But all these cannot 'undo' that 'silence' which is tied fast to her 'sense'. All other sound is irrelevant, compared with this intimately known absence of sound. Poems cannot shape it into meaning or enter it as a substitute. Instead, it lies below all poems like a negation of everything they might say.

Once again, Elizabeth Barrett denies that poems can express or break the silence of the dead. Instead, that silence shames her out of poetry. Against it, she lists the motifs of inspiration a poet might use: the voices of 'viols', 'pipes', 'poets', 'nightingales', 'angels'. Her imagination is ready with well-tried figures to take the place of the one 'belovèd voice' which has gone missing. But all these are weak, 'nay, none of these', and the poem comes round again to the same unimaginable 'pause'. In that 'pause', which is the poet's last word, the voice of Christ might perhaps avail.

These elegiac sonnets are written with an acute sense of contradiction between having 'power' to write, but none to change the facts of Bro's death. The shame of this actual powerlessness cannot then be overcome by the power of words. The silence of Elizabeth's unspoken grief runs like a strong undertow to these poems, which are won from its current with evident effort. This silence is not a superior form of expressiveness, which gives to language a reach beyond itself; it is simply a negation. The real 'desert place' of grief makes the poet's 'high-faned hills' distant and irrelevant. Grief, for Elizabeth Barrett, is the blank side of writing, which shames and contradicts the high revelations of poetry.

The desert landscapes of these sonnets seem like a hard resolution of the choice later offered in *Casa Guidi Windows*:

> Unless we choose
> To look back to the hills behind us spread,
> The plains before us sadden and confuse;
> If orphaned, we are disinherited.

The grieving sonnets of 1844, which are Elizabeth Barrett's first mature and underivative poems, in a sense embrace the condition of being 'orphaned' and 'disinherited' of 'the Dead'. Creative power comes to this poet, in spite of herself, from the cruel and terrible absence of the beloved. The desert 'plains' are the authentic landscapes of her consciousness, for in these landscapes there are no lingering spirits of the dead, and no names or inscriptions with which to recall them. From this place of imaginative disinheritance, she rejects as inappropriate 'the hills behind', and with them all the comforting and uplifting motifs of poetic inspiration. She chooses, instead, to stay in the saddening and confusing 'plains', in the 'desert place' of 'tombs', in order to embrace the 'Full desertness' of the soul which will not mitigate, in poetry, the fact of its grief and of its loss.

Chapter Five

'How do I love thee?': The Woman's Right to Say

'I love your verses with all my heart, dear Miss Barrett,' was the first sentence of Robert Browning's first letter to Elizabeth. Some lines later he repeated the point: 'I do, as I say love these books with all my heart—and I love you too.' Elizabeth received this letter in January 1845. She had never met Robert Browning, but she knew and liked his poetry, and had gone so far as to mention his name in 'Lady Geraldine's Courtship', alongside the names of Wordsworth and Tennyson. The poem had lately appeared in the 1844 two-volume edition of her *Poems*. Clearly, however, Robert Browning was not just politely replying to the compliment. He also wrote that 'so into me has it gone, and part of me has it become, this great living poetry of yours' (*Letters: 1845–1846*, I, 3). This first letter carries the conviction of a real admiration for Elizabeth Barrett's poetry, even if, in retrospect, it has an air of being speculative for romance.

That romance, as is well known, flourished—in spite of Mr Barrett's rule, in spite of Elizabeth's age and invalidism, and in spite of the subtler emotional obstacles caused by the still recent death of Bro. At first, Elizabeth refused to see her correspondent and they merely exchanged letters—several each week. At last, on 20 May, more than four months after that first enthusiastic missive, she allowed Robert to visit her. A day or two later he wrote her a hasty and ill-timed declaration of his feelings. Elizabeth was appalled and afraid. She immediately destroyed the letter and sent a deeply reproachful answer to it: 'you do not know what pain you give me in speaking so wildly . . . You have said some intemperate things' (I, 72). Robert's reply was clumsy and ungenerous. His letter broadly hints that she has read too much into his words, and he develops an ingeniously elaborate metaphor of his character, as a volcano with hidden cold depths, to prove the point. Of these depths, he asserts, outsiders remain ignorant, and even his poetry fails to communicate them: 'all my writings are purely dramatic as I am always anxious to say'. This characteristic pronouncement classes his over-intimate letter with all his other evasive 'dramatic' writings, and implicitly accuses Elizabeth of being too eager in her inferences. 'Will you not think me very brutal if I tell you I could almost smile at your misapprehension of what I meant to write?' (I, 74), he told her.

The brutally insulting pedantry of this whole letter clearly conceals hurt pride, and it is to Elizabeth's customary credit that she noticed the fact, and wrote back without any injury in her tone: 'I am quite as much ashamed of myself as I ought to be, which is not a little' (I, 78). However it is interesting that, many months later, she generalised the problem of male vanity in a letter to Robert, and sides with the women who are trapped by it:

The falseness and the calculations!—why how can you, who are *just, blame women* . . when you must know what the 'system' of man is towards them,—& of men not ungenerous otherwise? Why are women to be blamed if they act as if they had to do with swindlers? . . . And your 'honourable men', the most loyal of them . . . is it not a rule with them . . . to force a woman to stand committed in her affections . . . before *they* risk the pin-prick to their own personal pitiful vanities? (I, 341)

Whether she was also remembering that early letter, in which the author saved his male vanity by using the double-back tactics of an emotional swindler, remains to be guessed.

This early misunderstanding was succeeded by others, and the so-called love letters often make hard reading for their emotional ingenuity and argumentativeness. One constant source of disagreement between the lovers concerned their relative merits as poets. Each insisted on being the lesser artist, and exalted the other with proud and demanding certainty. For instance, in his disingenuous explanation of Elizabeth's blunder, Robert ends by stressing, nonetheless, her inherent superiority: 'I really believe you to be my superior in many respects, and feel uncomfortable till *you* see that, too—since I hope for your sympathy & assistance' (I, 74). It is she who slyly points out that this is hardly 'an apposite moment for you to talk, even "dramatically," of my "superiority" to you' (I, 78). Yet such praise was to dog her for much of their courtship. Robert insisted on placing her above himself, both as a poet and as a person, with the curious corollary that from her high place she could best give him 'sympathy & assistance'. His praise of her very often comes round to thoughts of his own work. When she sketches for him her intentions to write a long, contemporary poem, for instance, he eagerly takes up her proposal with 'it is what I have been all my life intending to do, and now shall be much, much nearer doing' (I, 36). Elizabeth's praise, on the other hand, tends towards a more generous, if exaggerated, praise of the man. He is, she declares, ' "masculine" to the height' (I, 9), and to this pedestal of masculinity she continues to assign him. A year later she writes: 'My own beloved!—you should have my soul to stand on if it could make you stand higher' (I, 532). The imagery of heights and depths, in which both were proficient, is clearly an imagery of subtle competition between them to be the lover, not the beloved.

Betty Miller claims that this competition resulted in Elizabeth's defeat, and in her 'consenting . . . to the process of beatification'.[1] But if this was true in life, it was not true in her poetry. Here, her love explores a language of self-abasement that is paradoxically proud of its imaginative rights. 'Oh—I hold to my rights,' she declared in a letter, 'though you overcome me in most other things. And it is my right to love you better than I could do if I were more worthy to be loved by you' (I, 565). The reasoning is contorted but triumphant. She will not yield her right to be the less worthy, but therefore stronger, lover. She clings with proud tenacity to the role of loving rather than of being loved.

Behind this struggle to be the subject of love rather than its object, it is possible to detect the old poetic need to find a muse, a high, beloved Other, who will inspire, as well as love, a love poetry: 'Oh—you do not understand how with an unspeakable wonder, an astonishment which keeps me from drawing breath, I look to this Dream, & "see your face as the face of an angel," and fear for the vanishing' (I, 532). It was Elizabeth who wrote this. Very often in these letters she playfully adapts the old figures for the beloved to fit

Robert. 'Talk of Sirens', she writes, 'there must be some masculine ones ... to justify this voice I hear' (I, 540) He is to her an angel or a siren—a rare apparition which she hardly trusts to stay. Certainly, the 'process of beatification' was not on one side only. Elizabeth's new-found right to love was also a right to claim the object of that love for her poetry, as she had claimed the figures of her father, her mother and even, in a sense, her brother, before. 'You shall see some day at Pisa what I will not show you now' (II, 892), she hinted darkly.

It is possible to generalise that, until the composition of the *Sonnets from the Portuguese* in 1845 and 1846, most of Elizabeth Barrett's love poems are poems of failed romance. By contrast to the lover-like attraction of the father and the moral sternness of the mother, the figure of the betrothed is a weak antagonist. Whether as a result of a streak of Gothic fatalism or of some opposite emotional pull, most of her early love poems end in death or desertion. One intriguing ballad, written before Elizabeth's meeting with Robert, reveals how much of a change that love worked on her imagination.

'The Romance of the Swan's Nest' (1844) tells the story of Ellie, who dreams of a lover on a 'red-roan steed' (44),[2] and of how he will win her hand by brave deeds. She dreams her archaic romance each day by the river-side. However, there is another reason for her desire for a gallant knight. Ellie has a secret which she will tell to no other; which is the existence of a 'swan's nest among the reeds' (24). But when, one day, she goes to look as usual, there has been a violent change: 'Lo, the wild swan had deserted,/And a rat had gnawed the reeds!' (95–6).

The last verse of the poem upsets all the usual romance conventions:

Ellie went home sad and slow.

95

> If she found the lover ever,
>> With his red-roan steed of steeds,
> Sooth I know not; but I know
> She could never show him—never,
>> That swan's nest among the reeds!
>> (97–102)

The surprise is not that the lover is unfaithful or that he never arrives; it is that he becomes unimportant: 'Sooth I know not'. Whatever strong woman's knowledge the nest represents—whether it be the failure of maternal instincts, the desire for freedom, or some more sinister idea of sexual violation—it is a knowledge which cannot now be shared with the knight of romance. It remains ambiguous whether the nest is destroyed by the swan's desertion or by the rat's attack on it; but in either case, this new realism of the imagination makes knights and love-tokens pale into insignificance. In the end Ellie keeps her secret, and loses her dream of a lover.

The poem seems to advocate, in the place of romantic love, some greater woman's knowledge of desertion or violation. This realism is characteristic of Elizabeth Barrett's own attitude to the sexual conventions of her time. The language of romance, she knew, often masked a real social injustice and inequality between the sexes. She was perfectly aware, for instance, of the notorious double standard, that it is 'relatively less excusable, for a woman endowed with modesty . . . to be immoral, than it is for a man to obey the nature of his sex,'[3] as one Victorian man put it. Against this accepted difference in standards she protested vigorously: 'The censure "*with a difference*" extended by our gracious world to male & female offenders—the crushing into dust for the woman—and the "oh you naughty man" ism for the betrayer—appears to me an injustice which cries upwards from the earth' (*MRM*, I, 295). Her abhorrence of any 'mythology of special regard'[4] towards women is shown in her reaction to her friend, Mr Hunter, who, it seems, had some designs on her hand. She told Miss Mitford that 'he talks epigrams about the sin & shame of those divine angels, called women, daring to tread in the dust of a multitude, when they ought to be minding their clouds.' She adds that 'the feeling is all to be analyzed into contempt of the sex' (*MRM*, III, 81). Although, years later, she would take Robert for an ' "angel" ', all her life she protested with indignation against that attitude of men which rarefies women into the useless objects of pious or poetic veneration.

It is interesting that the critics who are guilty of precisely this kind of veneration are those who, in the first decades of the twentieth century, praised the *Sonnets from the Portuguese* above all Barrett Browning's work. The idea of a woman writing love poems elicits from them a flood of sentimental approbation which, like Mr Hunter, 'talks epigrams . . . about divine angels'. The poems are praised at this time for the manifestly bad reason that they are true to life. 'The appeal of the Sonnets lies chiefly . . . in their evident truthfulness',[5] writes one critic in 1928; and in the same year another asserts that these poems have 'the authority of a fact'.[6] The fact in question is the womanly love of the author, which gains the critics' unrestrained approval, but which can also be analysed into contempt of the poet. For it is not as a love poet that Barrett Browning is praised, but as a representative of 'woman'. As a result, she is cunningly and predictably turned into the passive object rather than the active subject of love. 'This was the work that Mrs. Browning was born into the world to do—better than any man could do—to read to the full God's meaning when He made woman's heart,' wrote Eric Robertson in 1883. In 1928 Osbert Burdett was still writing in the same vein: 'She was feminine to the marrow, and only became a complete poet when she put her woman's response to his love into her verse.'[8] The ideal of womanliness, which somehow validates the writing of these poems, is subtly presented as a passive and reflective ideal. In the first statement, it is God who writes; the poet merely *reads* his 'meaning'. In the second, it is Robert who loves; she merely *responds* to it. This circumlocution somehow excludes the one thing Barrett Browning was so conscious of doing—of writing poems to express her *'right'* to love.

More recent criticism has understandably reacted against this veneration of the woman, and against the poems which provoked it. Alethea Hayter is embarrassed by what she regards as the biographical truth of the *Sonnets*;[9] Feit Diehl finds them 'often sentimental' and 'overly self-deprecating';[10] while Gilbert and Gubar register the poems' ideological disfavour by omitting any mention of them. The declared or implicit embarrassment of recent critics is itself the object of attack in one fine article by Dorothy Mermin, which discusses the way the *Sonnets* follow in a tradition of 'amatory poetry', but make deliberate 'painful dislocations' in its 'conventions'.[11]

To write a sonnet sequence is of course to trespass on a male domain. Dante, Petrarch, Sidney and Shakespeare are the eminent 'grandfathers' of this predominantly male line, and Barrett Browning is one of the first granddaughters. She thus enters into a tradition in which the roles are sexually delineated: there is the man who speaks, and there is the woman who is admired, described, cajoled and pleaded with from a distance. The woman is the high object who inspires both love and poetry, but who remains generally unmoved by both— thus, of course, ensuring their continuation. Barrett

Browning must not only reverse the roles, but she must also be sensitive to the fact that Robert was a lover and a poet in his own right, and disinclined to be cast in the role of the superior muse. His need for *her* to play that part is a need to which his letters bear ample witness. As a result, she takes care in these poems not to disturb the precarious balance of their imagination of each other, and a principle of equality in the best of the *Sonnets* is delicately preserved. It is in a faintly humorous and playful relation with the object of her heart's affection and her pen's praise that she maintains this fine balance of literary power.

Once again Barrett Browning finds herself, as a woman, repudiating the usual source of inspirational aid—the aid of the beautiful, silent, unrequiting muse—and tactfully imagining in her place a male figure who is her equal both as a poet and a lover. The 'name' of that lover 'moves right' (Sonnet VII) in all her poems' words, and gives those words their value. But at the same time she protects the figure of Robert from being simply the object of her verse. On the one hand, she leans her writing on the idea of his 'name', which thus lends its authority to her art; but on the other hand, she seeks to exclude Robert from any verbal gallantry or admiration which would make him a passive recipient of her love. The politics of subject and object, she knew too well, often served to turn women into useless 'divine angels', fit only to languish in a 'Book of Beauty' (*MRM*, III, 81) written by men. Therefore, she does not simply reverse the sexual roles; she disturbs them, either by interchanging her images of Robert, or else by protectively excluding him altogether from the strong and self-sufficient atmosphere of her love. Once again, the figure of the muse is a figure which this woman poet prefers to do without.

One of the ways in which she exempts Robert from such a role is by stressing the inner rather than the outer motivation for her writing, and thus stressing, forcefully and self-consciously, the woman's impulse to love and to speak:

> Yet, love, mere love, is beautiful indeed
> And worthy of acceptation. Fire is bright,
> Let temple burn, or flax; an equal light
> Leaps in the flame from cedar-plank or weed:
> And love is fire. And when I say at need
> *I love thee* . . . mark! . . . *I love thee*—in thy sight
> I stand transfigured, glorified aright,
> With conscience of the new rays that proceed
> Out of my face toward thine. There's nothing low
> In love, when love the lowest: meanest creatures
> Who love God, God accepts while loving so.
> And what I *feel*, across the inferior features
> Of what I *am*, doth flash itself, and show
> How that great work of Love enhances Nature's.
>
> (Sonnet X)

On the one hand, the poet offers her love to the beloved as one of the 'meanest creatures' to a God. But on the other hand, she reaches his level in being 'transfigured, glorified' by that love. To see only the self-deprecation of her confessed unworthiness is to miss the proud assertion of her accompanying rights, 'to love you better than I could do if I were more worthy to be loved by you.' It is from this strength of feeling that the *Sonnets* derive their strength of speech. The passage from one to the other needs no mediating worthy object. Simply by loving, the speaker learns to 'say at need/*I love thee* . . . mark! . . . *I love thee*—' with unashamed and unrequiring directness. To this declaration of her feelings, which is also a declaration of her right to speak about them, there is no need of an answer. The poem does not invoke the presence or the attention or the reciprocity of the loved object in order to be 'worthy'. Instead, it confirms its meaning independently. Simply by *saying*—'when I say at need'—the speaker brings about her own transformation in her lover's 'sight'. She has no need of his eyes to be 'transfigured'; the change comes from within.

It is interesting that in this sonnet she slips into the customary hagiographic mode, which describes the woman as a shining presence, her face raying out beauty like light. As Dorothy Mermin points out, 'the speaker casts herself not only as the poet who loves, speaks, and is traditionally male, but also as the silent, traditionally female beloved.'[12] However, even as she presents herself as the visual object of the poem, like some Beatrice or Laura, she is, grammatically, still the subject:

> I stand transfigured, glorified aright,
> With conscience of the new rays that proceed
> Out of my face toward thine.

Not only is this visible change the effect of her own speech; it is also a change of which she remains strongly *conscious*. She remains, from within, the mistress of her own effects. 'With conscience of the new rays' suggests an almost immodest awareness of the power of her own desire, and contains in its small compass a large argument for differing from the norm. To be unselfconscious is very often, in Victorian literature, a sign of sexual innocence and moral worth. In *Middlemarch*, for instance, Rosamund Vincy's self-mirroring personality is discreditably contrasted to Dorothea Brooke's self-forgetting moral generosity. In *Ruth*, Mrs Gaskell insists on the innocence of her heroine by repeatedly describing her as 'unconscious' of the effect she has on others. This innocence leads, however, by a sentimental logic of the imagination, to the apotheosised picture of Ruth on her death-bed, where she is finally and indisputably proved innocent because she is without any consciousness at all. This moral commonplace, that only the woman without consciousness of self is sexually pure, tends to reinforce the status of the woman as an object of sexual appreciation rather than a subject. Barrett Browning, however, portrays herself as both conscious and self-conscious in this poem. She is conscious of the power of her love and also of the beauty of her face.

Unwilling to portray Robert as a desirable object, Elizabeth Barrett Browning plays at being both subject and object herself, and thus in a cunning way protects him by exclusion. She is herself the subject who loves and who says so, and she is herself the object who is 'transfigured' by her own desire. Once again, she is as she was in 'The Lost Bower', both poet and muse. The effect of this confusion is one of verbal self-sufficiency and self-confidence. The beloved is there, but he is not exactly needed. What is needed is that the poet herself should have the courage to speak: 'And when I say at need/ *I love thee* . . .' It is from that needing to 'say' that her transformation comes.

[margin: Conclusion]

The idea of love as a transforming and inspiring power has a long history in literature. But it does not have a long history as the prerogative of the woman. In particular, it is not her part to speak of it. Yet it is this brave, even brazen, confidence of her right to speak of love which characterises Barrett Browning's *Sonnets.* That she was well aware of the conventions of Victorian courtship is clear from the letter defending the circumspection and silence forced on women by the emotional swindling of men. The *Sonnets,* however, in

their very emotional straightforwardness, seem to
protest against that calculating modesty, which really
leaves women weak and silent:

> How do I love thee? Let me count the ways.
> I love thee to the depth and breadth and height
> My soul can reach, when feeling out of sight
> For the ends of Being and ideal Grace.
> I love thee to the level of everyday's
> Most quiet need, by sun and candle-light.
> I love thee freely, as men strive for Right;
> I love thee purely, as they turn from Praise.
> I love thee with the passion put to use
> In my old griefs, and with my childhood's faith.
> I love thee with a love I seemed to lose
> With my lost saints,—I love thee with the breath,
> Smiles, tears, of all my life!—and, if God choose,
> I shall but love thee better after death.
>
> (Sonnet XLIII)

In some ways these poems, which seem so intimate
and so exclusively addressed to one person, in fact often
proclaim a self-sufficiency of love and of speech that
excludes the beloved altogether. This sonnet, famous
for its many appearances in anthologies—the one poem,
Carol Rumens remembers, which made her 'fusty
"Poems for Schools"/ . . . sweet as bridal blooms'[13]—simply incantates the old phrase 'I love thee'. This love is not
elicited by any special merit or beauty in the recipient,
who remains outside the poem's reference. Instead, the
speaker seems satisfied with a phrase merely. Its scope
becomes that of her whole life, its ambitions and its
banalities, its heights and its levels. This is a love so
confident of its object that it no longer needs it. Such
passion catches up a lifetime into significance, but leaves
out its first inspiration.

It is the mark of these woman's love poems that they do not struggle for the attention of the beloved; they do not plead or admire. Instead, they seem self-celebrating. They are not poems which seek to be heard in order to be justified; their justification is in the passion and effort of their own writing.

In those poems where the figure of the beloved actually appears, it is, as Dorothy Mermin points out, 'imaginatively transformed'.[14] Most commonly, Robert is portrayed as the successful singer or poet, in contrast to the speaker herself. He is the 'chief musician', a 'gracious singer of high poems'. She, by comparison, is a 'poor, tired, wandering singer', and 'an out of tune/ Worn viol'. This modesty trope is a strange one in poems which rejoice so in the impulse of their own composition, and evidently it is another attempt tactfully to confuse the roles of subject and object, poet and muse. Barrett Browning is, as a poet, acutely aware of the essentially disabling heights to which the object of love is relegated. The politics of subject and object in love poetry is traditionally a sexual politics, by which the woman is desirable and inspiring for being, herself, without desire and without language. The role of the object is to be still and dumb. Elizabeth was too conscious of the insult implicit in the imagination's desire for 'divine angels' to use the same tactics towards Robert. Yet, in the very act of writing love poems, she creates an object of that love, who is to some extent dispossessed of autonomy. One way in which she compensates for this is to portray Robert, not as still and silent as if in a picture, but as the greater singer who looks at *her*, and finds her to be merely old and tired. 'What hast *thou* to do/ With looking from the lattice-lights at me . . . ? she asks. She makes up for her own power of writing by claiming an inferiority of art, and by imagining herself as the one who is looked at. Thus, whether Robert is simply missing or imaginatively transformed into a singer and lover in his own right, he figures in these sonnets as a different kind of muse—a muse whose characteristic is to be neither properly seen nor named in these poems which nonetheless retain the sense of his real presence.

But there is another reason for this apparently 'self-deprecating' and sometimes exaggerated modesty about writing. In the first sonnet of the sequence, the 'Shape' that suddenly draws the speaker 'backward by the hair' is mistakenly greeted as '"Death"' not '"Love"'. The memory of Bro runs through these poems like an alternative inspiration that at times rivals the new. It is this consciousness of a grief which once devastated her imagination that in part shapes Barrett Browning's pessimistic presentation of herself. She is a 'poor, tired, wandering singer' because grief for the dead has exhausted her.

In Sonnet V, the heavy weight of this grief is revealed:

> I lift my heavy heart up solemnly,
> As once Electra her sepulchral urn
> And, looking in thine eyes, I overturn
> The ashes at thy feet. Behold and see
> What a great heap of grief lay hid in me,
> And how the red wild sparkles dimly burn
> Through the ashen greyness. If thy foot in scorn
> Could tread them out to darkness utterly,
> It might be well perhaps. But if instead
> Thou wait beside me for the wind to blow
> The grey dust up, . . . those laurels on thine head,
> O my Belovèd, will not shield thee so,
> That none of all the fires shall scorch and shred
> The hair beneath. Stand farther off then! go.
>
> (Sonnet V)

In Sophocles' *Electra* the heroine takes the urn which she thinks contains the ashes of her dead brother, Orestes. In fact, she is mistaken. But Barrett Browning's own heart truly contains the 'ashes' of her dead brother. It is that grief which threatens to put out all the sparks of passion in her.

The 'ashes' and 'sparkles' represent grief and love, which now contend for her heart. Grief has brought her near to death, but the small lights of passion that remain are still capable of being kindled again, by some west wind of poetry. These 'red wild sparkles' among the 'ashes', she warns her poet lover, if not firmly trodden down 'in scorn', will set light to his poet's hair. This Shelleyan imagery of ashes, sparks and wind is interesting because it gives the poem an undercurrent meaning which denies its surface modesty. The dim 'sparkles' of her dormant passion are associated with a fire that is not only love, but also poetry. 'Stand farther off then! go.' It is not only her passion which Robert has reason to fear, but also the expression of that passion in verse. Although a worn-out singer of elegies, her heart is still capable of catching fire; and if it does so, the resulting poetry will 'scorch and shred' the other poet's hair.

It is a witty and assured logic which leads from the memory of grief to this imagined threat that comes from her creativity. She tells her beloved: 'those laurels on thine head,/ O my Belovèd, will not shield thee so.' The warning is affectionate and good-natured. But the hidden connection between sparks and poetry shows the threat to be quite serious. The fire of her poetic heart will have designs not only on his hair, but also on his 'laurels'.

It was the sense of ashes in the heart, however, which made Robert's love for a long time hard to accept.

Elizabeth's old love for Bro passes like a shadowy double behind these poems, and she clings to the imagery of that love sometimes with a sad faithfulness:

> But I look on thee—on thee—
> Beholding, besides love, the end of love,
> Hearing oblivion beyond memory;
> As one who sits and gazes from above,
> Over the rivers to the bitter sea.
> (Sonnet XV)

Love tempts her away from her old loyalties, and the figure of Robert seems to interrupt her long vision back towards 'the bitter sea'. It is clear that the place of Bro is being supplanted in her imagination by this new figure: '"Not Death, but Love"'. But the harsh superimposition of love on grief in the *Sonnets* betrays the extent to which the role of these beloved men is the same. However reluctantly or tactfully she expresses it, they are both objects of Barrett Browning's imaginative desire to write. Yet they feature in her poetry as presences which are ultimately separate and different from poems. These poems take shape round the allowed absence of the muse.

It is not only as 'chief musician' or as 'gracious singer of high poems' that Robert is pictured, however. In Sonnet XXXVII, for instance, Barrett Browning begins by thanking him for having rescued her from the 'bitter sea' of her past, and then slyly admits how far she has mistaken his image:

> Pardon, oh, pardon, that my soul should make,
> Of all that strong divineness which I know
> For thine and thee, an image only so
> Formed of the sand, and fit to shift and break.
> It is that distant years which did not take

Thy sovranty, recoiling with a blow,
Have forced my swimming brain to undergo
Their doubt and dread, and blindly to forsake
Thy purity of likeness and distort
Thy worthiest love to a worthless counterfeit:
As if a shipwrecked Pagan, safe in port,
His guardian sea-god to commemorate,
Should set a sculptured porpoise, gills a-snort
And vibrant tail, within the temple-gate.

(Sonnet XXXVII)

Wordsworth's wish to be 'A Pagan suckled in a creed outworn',[15] and so have some vision at least of the old sea-gods, is remembered in this sonnet which movingly mingles the shipwreck of Barrett Browning's past life with her new hope and love. But in this poem she also humorously imagines a mistake. In one of her letters she reassures Robert that 'I never bowed down to any of the false gods—I know the gold from the mica' (*Letters: 1845–1846*, I,532). But in the confusion of shipwreck and from a still 'swimming brain', this speaker enshrines 'a sculptured porpoise' instead of the true god. The joke works both against her own habit of veneration and against the high object of that veneration. Robert is her 'guardian sea-god', and the image looks forward to the return of the 'sea-king' at the end of *Aurora Leigh*. But in her confused gratefulness, she rudely takes him for a 'porpoise'.

As so often in the *Sonnets*, the speaker claims to be making an apology for her weakness as a poet: she cannot match her images to the reality, she has missed the 'purity of likeness', or her desired object escapes her. But such humility is sometimes disingenuous. The surprising, vivid image of 'a sculptured porpoise, gills a-snort/ And vibrant tail' carries the imaginative conviction of the poem against the speaker's apologies. For all her acknowledgement of Robert's 'strong divineness', it is the shipwrecked Pagan's humble liveliness of imagination that inspires the poem. To mistake a brilliant 'fish' for an invisible god is a tactic that suits not only Barrett Browning's playful politics of love, but also her protective exclusion of the real object of her love from verbal travesty. Thus Robert remains, after all, a figure of ideal 'divineness', which the poet's pagan imagination crudely mimics.

It is not so much the imagery of these poems which makes them distinctive, but their playfully shifting registers of desire. The relationship between the speaker and her beloved is one which often confuses heights with levels, gods with fish. For all his declared superiority over her, as a laurelled poet or as a divine guardian, Robert is still quietly threatened with having his hair scorched or his divine image taken in vain. Yet because the poem intrudes itself as a distorting image of its object, it thus permits that object to remain in some sense autonomous and apart.

This sense of the beloved's absence is what makes the poem both strong and false:

> I think of thee!—my thoughts do twine and bud
> About thee, as wild vines, about a tree,
> Put out broad leaves, and soon there's nought to see
> Except the straggling green which hides the wood.
> Yet, O my palm-tree, be it understood
> I will not have my thoughts instead of thee
> Who art dearer, better! Rather, instantly
> Renew thy presence; as a strong tree should,
> Rustle thy boughs and set thy trunk all bare,
> And let these bands of greenery which insphere thee
> Drop heavily down,—burst, shattered, everywhere!
> Because, in this deep joy to see and hear thee

And breathe within thy shadow a new air,
I do not think of thee—I am too near thee.
                              (Sonnet XXIX)

As in the sonnets about grief, the reality is too dear to be traded for words. But although the impulse of the poem is to give the speaker's twining 'thoughts' in exchange for the real 'presence' which they hide, that exchange cannot be made until the poem is over. 'I do not think of thee—I am too near thee' is still a wish conditional on there being nothing more to write. Meanwhile, the poem's greenery makes 'nought to see' where the figure of Robert should stand. It forces the object out of sight and out of words. For as long as the speaker thinks her poem, she must miss the presence which supports it. Yet the alternative is that the object renews its 'presence' by depriving her of the power of her poetic art. 'I do not think of thee—I am too near thee' would be the end of poems if she were truly content to be in Robert's 'shadow'. Instead, the exchange of her thoughts for thoughtlessness is one she can afford to make, having written the poem. The self-renouncing modesty of her intention is undermined by the self-conscious evidence of all the poem's 'straggling green'.

Thus for all their self-abasement, the *Sonnets* betray a knowledge of the power of their own writing, even where they seem to wage a struggle against that writing.[16] Barrett Browning knows that to be mistress of 'the power at the end of my pen' is to enter into a political game of subject and object in which the one is gained at the other's expense. For all her protestations, she does not, in *practice*, give up her woman's right to speak:

And wilt thou have me fashion into speech
The love I bear thee, finding words enough,

And hold the torch out, while the winds are rough,
Between our faces, to cast light on each?—
I drop it at thy feet. I cannot teach
My hand to hold my spirit so far off
From myself—me—that I should bring thee proof
In words, of love hid in me out of reach.
Nay, let the silence of my womanhood
Commend my woman-love to thy belief,—
Seeing that I stand unwon, however wooed,
And rend the garment of my life, in brief,
By a most dauntless, voiceless fortitude,
Lest one touch of this heart convey its grief.

(Sonnet XIII)

Here Barrett Browning declares that the mark of 'woman-love' is naturally womanhood's 'silence'. She begins by denying her own power to 'fashion into speech' those feelings which lie too far within her to be coolly extracted in words. The woman poet protests, therefore, that she cannot write of these things.

However, the reasons are not the expected ones. It is not the impropriety of speech which daunts her, nor is it any fear of being rashly committed in her affections before her sexual adversary. The 'silence of my womanhood' which she recommends is not a sexual political tactic—a form of required modesty—nor is it some Romantic spiritualising of a love which surpasses words. Instead, such 'silence' proves to be merely a generous kind of restraint, for reasons that reveal not the impotence, but the very force of her words. She asks the beloved if she dare to 'hold the torch out, while the winds are rough,/ Between our faces, to cast light on each?' It is not that she fears to reveal *herself*, but that she fears to bring a torch to light both their faces, 'while the winds are rough'. This is the image of a threatening fire again. The speaker fears to scorch her beloved with

111

poetry fanned by rough winds of passion. Those winds would make the flame uncontrollable. The 'torch' of her words is an instrument not so much of light, to reveal, as of fire, to burn. This is why she would 'drop it' at her beloved's 'feet'.

Behind the poem's apparent modesty, there is a subtly immodest confidence in the power of her woman's words to flame and burn wildly. To protect the beloved, therefore, she will keep 'the silence' of 'womanhood'. This 'silence' is in fact a 'voiceless fortitude', that comes near to breaking her with self-restraint. It is a 'fortitude' to protect not herself, therefore, but her beloved, 'Lest one touch of this heart convey its grief.' The poem falls into phrases that seem to recommend a conventional principle of restraint and propriety in women. It seems to say that the place of 'woman-love' is with 'the silence of . . . womanhood'. But what the poem cunningly tells is that those womanly principles are only a way of protecting the beloved from the threatening power of woman-words. Those she withholds, sensibly, 'while the winds are rough'.

Meanwhile, however, this sonnet, like all the others, contradicts the convention of woman's silence. Barrett Browning, although she may protest her own literary inability and more fit silence, in practice does not forbear to write poem after poem about her 'woman-love'. She is still the lover, the sonneteer, the subject of her poems, and she borrows for her speech a male literary form which itself traditionally emphasised 'the silence of . . . womanhood' as the high required silence of the muse.

She thus writes her own sonnet sequence with the perceptiveness and generosity of a usurper of power in the poetic politics of love, but also with an often justified awareness of the strength of her writing. The *Sonnets from the Portuguese* are powerful as a declaration of the woman's right to be, not silent, but rather confidently self-expressive. This right is the real inspiration of their writing.

Chapter Six

'If orphaned, we are disinherited':
The Making of the Poet

Barrett Browning first projected the composition of
Aurora Leigh as early as 1844. She wrote to her cousin and
friend, John Kenyon, of her wish to write another poem
like 'Lady Geraldine's Courtship'. Such a poem would be
longer and more ambitious, but similarly 'compre-
hending the aspect and manners of modern life, and
flinching at nothing of the conventional' (*Kenyon*, I, 204).
Some months later, she embellished this first description in a letter to Miss Mitford: 'And now tell me,—where
is the obstacle to making as interesting a story of a poem
as of a prose work . . . Conversations & events, why may
they not be given as rapidly & passionately & lucidly in
verse as in prose—'. Her main intention in such a work,
she stresses, is 'to go on, & touch this real everyday life
of our age, & hold it with my two hands'. She adds,
confidently: 'I want to write a poem of a new class'
(*MRM*, III, 49).

A year later, she had not yet begun this poem but was
still contemplating its composition. She informed

Robert that 'my chief *intention* just now is the writing of a sort of novel-poem . . . running into the midst of our conventions, & rushing into drawing-rooms & the like "where angels fear to tread"; & so, meeting face to face & without mask the Humanity of the age' (*Letters: 1845–1846*, I, 31). The poem she outlines will be crusadingly modern, iconoclastic and outspoken, and it will contain, as well as philosophical digressions on the age, the popular interest of a story. Barrett Browning did not begin to write *Aurora Leigh* until after her marriage and the birth of Pen. It belongs, therefore, to some of the happiest years of her life—years in which she became a wife, mother, cosmopolitan traveller and tireless observer of the revolutionary events in Europe after 1848. It was published in 1856, a few months before the death of Mr Barrett.

In its exuberant and fierce commitment to the present, *Aurora Leigh* indeed succeeds in being 'a poem of a new class'. Not only does Barrett Browning unflinchingly relate a story of modern life, highly charged and melodramatic as it is; she also successfully promulgates a message of literary contemporaneity which other writers of the time enthusiastically welcomed. She repudiates the habit of nostalgia which tempts the Victorian poet with the glamour of the past, and from this new sense of the present she develops a crusadingly female poetics. The heroine of the work is a poet herself, who writes the story of her life and literary success as one example of the general cause of women's emancipation and independence. The 'real everyday life of our age' which Barrett Browning confronts in *Aurora Leigh* is mainly the 'real everyday life' of women, in all its small domestic detail; and it is from this specific bias that she derives a theory of women's writing as contemporary, combative and self-sufficient. However, it is one of the strengths and merits of the work that it also traces the hidden personal cost of this achievement.

Between 1846, the year of Elizabeth's marriage, and 1857, the year of Mr Barrett's death, there was no word from him. Although Elizabeth wrote many pleading letters to the father who might once have bound her to him 'hand and foot' (*Kenyon*, I, 291), his silence was unremitting. On one visit to England, in 1851, her continuing hopes for reconciliation must have been finally dashed by his abrupt return of all her past letters, unopened. Yet, in spite of this characteristically unsparing rigidity, the cherished ideal of her father continued to haunt his daughter, and all the rich compensations of her new life continued to be measured, in a sense, against the fact of his silence. 'All her life [the daughter] may longingly seek that lost state of plenitude and peace',[1] de Beauvoir writes.

In *Aurora Leigh*, Barrett Browning builds her hopeful political message of independence and equality for women upon a hidden last quest for the father. That quest is mapped in the sub-plot of the story, and its end is realised in Aurora's final knowledge and acceptance of her 'orphaned' and 'disinherited' state. Thus, it is not only a literary, but also a personal nostalgia for the past which this poet must repudiate in order to fulfil her own high specifications for poetry. In order to write 'a poem of a new class' which touches the 'real everyday life of our age', Barrett Browning finally dispossesses herself of the powerful figure of the father, both in fact and in imagination. The 'feminist' conviction of *Aurora Leigh* grows out of this harsh emotional and imaginative loss.

There are three interrelated stories in the work. First, there is the story of Aurora's life. Born of an Italian mother and English father, Aurora is early orphaned of them both, and is reared by an English aunt. She comes in time to reject the oppressive, puritanical education of this aunt, as well as the more insidiously oppressive offer of marriage by her rich cousin, Romney. She chooses instead to live alone in London and to earn her living by writing. Finally, through a series of novelistic detours, she returns to Italy to find that literary success and love are not irreconcilable after all. Secondly, there is the story of Marian Erle, the working-class girl to whom Romney also proposes, in a high-minded attempt to match his practice to his socialistic theories. Marian comes under the evil influence of the aristocratic Lady Waldemar, who persuades her to desert Romney on the very day of the wedding and to escape to France. Here she is raped in a brothel, gives birth to a child, and is finally discovered by Aurora, with whom she goes to Italy to live in an alternative liaison of women. It is there that Romney finds them both, when, defeated and broken by the practice of his misplaced philanthropical ideals, he too arrives in Italy. Thirdly, there is the underlying story of Aurora the poet, who is a scarcely disguised representative of Barrett Browning herself. This is an autobiography of literary development, which takes the form of a poetic quest for two figures whose presences shape Aurora's growth as a poet. It is this third story which holds the key to Barrett Browning's purpose and achievement in *Aurora Leigh*.

The main plot of the work is that of an improbable melodramatic romance interlaced with long philosophical digressions on the art and spirit of the age. In its general references and outline, this plot is indebted, as Cora Kaplan has shown,[2] to a large number of other nineteenth-century works, among which the most prominent are Madame de Staël's *Corinne* and Charlotte Brontë's *Jane Eyre*. The sub-plot, however, remains characteristically and underivatively Barrett Browning's own. It traces Aurora's quest for two figures, whom she seeks with the lover-like urgency of a poet seeking her muse. The first of these is the father, whose presence is movingly and anxiously solicited, as if in a last appeal by the daughter whose strong consciousness of disinheritance had come cruelly true in life. It is this appeal to the past which the poem ultimately rejects and supersedes, in order to free Aurora for her second quest—for a sister.

> Of writing many books there is no end;
> And I who have written much in prose and verse
> For others' uses, will write now for mine,—
> Will write my story for my better self . . .
>
> (I, 1-4)

Aurora Leigh begins with a declaration of literary purpose which the whole poem then supports. Aurora has already 'written much in prose and verse', but this, her latest book, will be a different story, which answers to the requirements of her 'better self'. The fact that the poem opens with a fanfare on the theme of writing reveals the extent to which this is the story of that self's writing. Beneath its flamboyant plot, *Aurora Leigh* is a woman's 'Prelude', which is concerned to chart the origins and development of the woman poet's mind. These origins are not, however, nurturing Wordsworthian presences of nature, but, true to Barrett Browning's Victorian and daughterly preoccupations, they are the heroine's actual parents. It is these whom she invokes at the start: 'But still I catch my mother at her post/ Beside the nursery door' (I, 15-16), and then, more intimately: 'Still I sit and feel/ My father's slow hand, when she had left us both' (I, 19-20). These presences are so vivid to the speaker's imagination that the writing slips into a present tense of strongly nostalgic recuperation.

However, the very vividness of these memories of mother and father betrays the curiously apprehensive foreboding which prompts them. Aurora does not simply commemorate those first powerful influences on her life; she also thinks, in the present tense:

> O my father's hand,
> Stroke heavily, heavily the poor hair down,
> Draw, press the child's head closer to thy knee!
> I'm still too young, too young, to sit alone.
>
> (I, 25-8)

'His hand would not lie so heavily,' Elizabeth once wrote of her own father, 'without a pulse in it' (*Letters: 1845-1846*, II, 882). The image of the father's hand in her poetry is one which, as Virginia Steinmetz points out,[3] often links strong human love and hard, God-like authority. This first description of the father in *Aurora Leigh* clearly draws on the contradictions in the character of that real father. His hand is a comfort to the child, but it is also unthinkingly heavy.

However, this description of the father is already loaded with intimations of change. The generalised present tense of these first passages subtly mixes fact and memory, event and premonition. The child who thinks, 'I'm still too young ,too young, to sit alone', does so in the same grammatical time as Aurora who writes it many years later, and this trick of perspective carries an emotional and imaginative significance which the whole poem confirms. The sense of impending death comes earlier in the speaker's consciousness than it does in the poem's narrative, and thus it impresses the adult's foreboding on the chronology of events. Furthermore, it suggests a connection which will recur, with striking frequency, throughout the work. Although, in the plot, Aurora's father dies when she is thirteen, in Barrett

Browning's consciousness he dies as soon as she begins to write.

This connection is evident in the apposition of lines which follows:

> I'm still too young, too young, to sit alone.
> I write.
>
> (I, 28–9)

The declaration 'I write' interrupts the sequence of events in a way that is highly suggestive. In the poet's imagination, the idea of losing her father and of having, therefore, 'to sit alone', leads by some swift association of ideas to the act of writing. Barrett Browning's insistence on the verb 'to write' in these first paragraphs of *Aurora Leigh*[4] goes with a premonition of being dispossessed of a mother and a father. The very break between the first and second paragraphs, like the famous 'awkward break'[5] noted by Virginia Woolf in *Jane Eyre*, is resonant with possible connections. The one connection which so much of Barrett Browning's work corroborates is that between the fear of being 'orphaned' and the confidence of being able to write.

After this richly revealing confusion of ideas in the first passages of *Aurora Leigh*, Book I relates in a more orderly way the deaths of Aurora's mother and father, and the child's subsequent exile from her homeland, Italy, to her father's land, England. The mother dies first. 'She was weak and frail' (I, 33), Aurora tells, in words which recall Barrett Browning's descriptions of her real mother in her letters. This death is then obscurely linked with the mothering role: 'The mother's rapture slew her' (I, 35). It is not a literal death in childbirth which is referred to here, but some vague excess of motherly experience. All Elizabeth Barrett's

120

old distrust and antagonism towards the figure of the mother is then vented in Aurora's confused, horrified attitude to her mother's portrait. As Barbara Gelpi has shown, this portrait becomes the focus of all the child's wild and frightened imaginings about 'womanhood itself'.[6] In the firelight, the white of the woman's skin and the red of her ballroom gown contrast luridly: 'That swan-like supernatural white life/ Just sailing upward from the red stiff silk' (I, 139–40). The portrait then draws the child's thoughts into a region of shifting and uncertain images of woman: it is 'by turns/ Ghost, fiend, and angel, fairy, witch, and sprite' (I, 153–4), or else a 'Muse' (155), a 'Psyche' (156), a 'Medusa' (157), 'Our Lady of the Passion' (160), a 'Lamia' (161). These are all either threatening or tragically defeated figures of womanhood. Even the 'Muse' is not one to inspire poems, for she is about to be overcome by 'a dreadful Fate' (155). The Gothicism of this whole passage recalls the younger poet's profound anxiety of womanliness—an anxiety which, in her early ballads, turned the figure of the ghostly mother into a sometimes grotesque object of suspicion and fear.

Predictably, *Aurora Leigh* confirms that it is the father whose image dominates and inspires the daughter poet. Aurora relates that, after her mother's death:

> He left our Florence and made haste to hide
> Himself, his prattling child, and silent grief,
> Among the mountains above Pelago . . .
> (I, 109–11)

The 'prattling child' and the austerely 'silent' father make a strange company in the little mountain house. Their touchingly incongruous intimacy is not only, however, an authentic fact of the narrative; it is also a sign of what is to come. The idea of the father's 'silence' is one which soon acquires, not only the harsh authority of subsequent events, but also the subtle, guilty authority of an imaginative need.

Aurora tells:

> I was just thirteen,
> Still growing like the plants from unseen roots
> In tongue-tied Springs,—and suddenly awoke
> To full life and life's needs and agonies
> With an intense, strong, struggling heart beside
> A stone-dead father. Life, struck sharp on death,
> Makes awful lightning.
>
> (I, 205–11)

As has been pointed out, 'Aurora loses her mother at the Oedipal moment—age four—and her father as she attains the menarch.'[7] This timing of the father's death has an eerie deliberateness about it. It happens suddenly and inexplicably, without narrative justification; but it retains, nonetheless, some hidden connection with Aurora's awakening to 'full life'. The juxtaposition is cruel, but apposite. It may be that Elizabeth's own experience of her father's tyrannical opinions about 'the iniquity of love-affairs' (*Letters: 1845–1846*, II, 1072) lies behind this carefully timed literary death. Certainly, the passage strongly reinforces the connection made many years before in the ballads: it is the daughter's growth into womanhood, with all its wider physical and emotional needs, which signifies the loss of the father to her; she has ceased to be to him 'as if . . . a child'.

But there is another connection in the passage. It is not only the daughter's emotional development, but also her literary development which coincides with the father's death. The imagery of the passage confuses the two.

122

Aurora grows as if from 'roots/ In tongue-tied Springs' to find, beside the fact of her 'stone-dead father', her own 'intense, strong, struggling heart'. Such language recalls the early drama of 'The Tempest'. There is the same sudden juxtaposition of the 'struggling' protagonist and the dead man, and the same contrast between the desired self-expression of the one and the silence of the other. The very strength of life in Aurora provides a cruel contrast to, but also a subtle reason for, the father's death. 'Life, struck sharp on death,/ Makes awful lightning,' Barrett Browning writes. Such imagery carries an irresistible suggestion, not only of emotional violence, but also of literary exhilaration. Just as the daughter wakes to womanhood and self-expression, so the father, by some ruthless logic of the imagination, appears 'stone-dead'. So sharp is the clash between daughter and father that it seems like life won at the cost of death; like speech won from some profound subsconscious crime against that father, the 'familiar'. Out of this clash, however, comes poetry: 'lightning'.

But it is characteristic of *Aurora Leigh*, as of all Barrett Browning's work, to feel the loss behind its power, and to go on hearing the silence behind its speech. This is the legacy of the father muse. Aurora claims that the last word of her dying father was to ' "Love, my child, love, love!" ' (I, 212). However, the rest of the poem makes clear that the real legacy of the father to his poet daughter is a legacy to hear, behind all the new and varied sounds of her life, his powerful silence. It is that silence which fills her imagination with its harshly formative strength of contradiction. Thus, when the child Aurora is torn away from her Italian home and Nanny, it is 'with ears too full/ Of my father's silence to shriek back a word' (I, 227–8). It is not her father's last word to ' "love" ' which rings in her ears, but his last 'silence'.

Sandra Gilbert has argued that Aurora's subsequent struggle to survive is a struggle between 'two *paysages moralisés*, her mother country of Italy and her fatherland of England';[8] and she concludes that Aurora chooses the generous nurture and eroticism of Italy and rejects the 'patriarchal history'[9] represented by the father's tongue and country. But this ideological alignment fails to take into account the poem's movingly persistent quest for the lost father in the landscapes of *both* England and Italy. The significance of each of those places is a significance provided by the father's absence from them. Aurora's real choice is not so much one of motherland or fatherland, as it is the choice to survive in a world which, because of the father's absence, is all a desert. The story of her development and eventual independence as a woman and as a poet is a story wrung out of the emotionally and imaginatively realised fact that 'If orphaned, we are disinherited'.

Aurora first feels the meaning of her new orphaned state in the boat which takes her to England. She finds that 'the very sky' (I, 244) is

> Bedraggled with the desolating salt,
> Until it seemed no more that holy heaven
> To which my father went. All new and strange;
> The universe turned stranger, for a child.
>
> (I, 247–50)

The estranged and bewildered child finds that, with the loss of her father, the mark of the whole 'universe' is to be strange and bewildering. The sense of a 'holy heaven' which contains the presence of that father quickly fades before the literal 'desolating' grey of the real sky. Not only is there a new emptiness at the heart of things in

124

Aurora's consciousness; there is also a new pressing and oppressive fullness. The obstructing reality of the actual sky takes the place of the 'holy heaven' of her child's faith. Just as in the grieving sonnets of 1844, the visionariness of 'stars and sun' is denied to the true mourners in the desert, so here, any consoling vision of 'heaven' is slowly usurped by the ordinary, separating fact of the sky. Skies, for Barrett Browning, are only a consolation to those whose loss is redeemable.

This contrast between poetic vision and ordinary sight is made again when Aurora describes her reluctant survival in England:

> I did not die. But slowly, as one in swoon,
> To whom life creeps back in the form of death,
> With a sense of separation, a blind pain
> Of blank obstruction, and a roar i' the ears
> Of visionary chariots which retreat
> As earth grows clearer . . . slowly, by degrees;
> I woke . . .
>
> (I, 559–65)

As she becomes accustomed to life again, the 'visionary chariots' seem to retreat with their beloved company of dead. They leave her with a form of sensory deprivation which is more like death than life, however: 'a blind pain/ Of blank obstruction, and a roar i' the ears'. All the new sights and sounds of the world to which Aurora once again awakes merely obtrude senselessly upon her imagination's desire for the other lost visions. Because she cannot see or hear her father in this world, its clarity is an oppression: an 'obstruction' of things and a 'roar' of sounds. With the father, the very imaginative resources of poetry seem to have been lost.

However, this exchange, which seems at first to be an exchange of life for death, of vision for dull sight, will become the principle of Barrett Browning's poetics. Aurora's gradual realisation of her 'orphaned' state is one which comes by finding that the salty, grey sky takes the place of the 'holy heaven', and that the clear 'earth' takes the place of 'visionary chariots'. The substitution of something loveless, hard and literal for the inspiring presence of the father is one on which the daughter's poetry must grow.

This principle of an exchange is suggested again in Book II. Aurora, now become a woman, encounters her cousin Romney in the garden in June, and there rejects his humiliating proposal of marriage. She accuses him of merely desiring a helpmate in his philanthropical projects, and of belittling her own different vocation of writing. Her description of that vocation, however, is one which still calls upon the memory of her father. She tells Romney:

> I too have my vocation,—work to do,
> The heavens and earth have set me since I changed
> My father's face for theirs . . .
>
> (II, 455–7)

The public message of *Aurora Leigh* is that the poet's work is as socially and politically beneficial as the philanthropist's. However, its private message is much less assured, and concerns the difficult, nearly unprecedented struggle of the woman poet to define her creativity. Barrett Browning's new poetics of contemporary commitment to the age is one which the woman achieves only through a principle of exchange or choice. Thus, Aurora admits that she has 'changed' her 'father's face' for a view of 'heavens and earth'. Although this new view is large and full, the father's absence makes it seem empty. 'Fatherlessness,' writes André Bleikasten, 'is not so much the absence of a relationship as a relationship to absence.'[10] The exchange of a father for the whole world, Barrett Browning knew, is in some ways an exchange of something for nothing. Nonetheless, it is that nothing which must nourish her imagination, and prepare it to meet 'this real everyday life of our age'. It is not her 'father's face' but the estranging 'heavens and earth' which have set Aurora to write poetry.

It is interesting that, at one point, Aurora distinguishes her bad early verses from her mature poems in terms of two different attitudes to the muse and of two different landscapes. In the first, she generalises:

> We call the Muse,—'O Muse benignant Muse,'—
> As if we had seen her purple-braided head,
> With the eyes in it, start between the boughs . . .
>
> (I, 980–2)

This easy confidence of finding the muse, like the lovely ladies of old, in a wood, is the mark of false poetry. True creativity, she knows now, comes in a very different place:

> In order to discover the Muse-Sphinx,
> The melancholy desert must sweep round,
> Behind you as before.—
>
> (I, 1020–2)

It is only in the 'melancholy desert', in the saddening and confusing plains that sweep, significantly, 'Behind' as well as 'before', that the muse is to be found. It is in the 'desert' of a world that harbours no beloved spirits of the past that Barrett Browning eventually discovers the muse of her contemporary 'feminist' epic.

But first, her quest for the lost father is pursued to its

Elizabeth Barrett Browning

end. That the death of her father is not just a narrative
strategy to liberate the heroine for life and love, as it is in
many Victorian novels, is shown by the reluctance with
which Aurora's imagination consents to that death. Her
struggle with the figure of the dead, forsaking father is
one which rivals in its emotional and poetic intensity the
struggle between herself and Romney. Thus, for
instance, at the moment when she rejects Romney's
proposal of marriage and asserts her own vocation to be
a poet, her thoughts turn to the presence which might
have rivalled Romney for love:

> I had a father! yes, but long ago—
> How long it seemed that moment. Oh, how far,
> How far and safe, God, dost thou keep thy saints
> When once gone from us! We may call against
> The lighted windows of thy fair June-heaven
> Where all the souls are happy,—and not one,
> Not even my father, look from work or play
> To ask, 'Who is it that cries after us,
> Below there, in the dusk?' Yet formerly
> He turned his face upon me quick enough,
> If I said 'Father.' Now I might cry loud;
> The little lark reached higher with his song
> Than I with crying. Oh, alone, alone,—
> Not troubling any in heaven, nor any on earth,
> I stood there in the garden, and looked up
> The deaf blue sky that brings the roses out
> On such June mornings.
>
> (II, 734–50)

Having defended her different vocation of writing,
Aurora is left to savour her loneliness. At the moment of
her triumphant self-assertion as a poet, she looks for her
father and finds him absent: 'Oh, alone, alone'.

This cry of despair is poignantly placed. Aurora has
just crowned herself, as if in imitation of Corinne, poet

laureate of the garden, and she has just proved to herself, and to Romney, that her ambition is strong and self-sufficient. But it is not so much from Romney's love that her self-sufficiency must be won, as from her father's. When she looks, the scene of her victory seems desolate and unresponsive. The 'fair June-heaven' is no different from the first heavy skies which the child saw on her journey to England. Both intrude themselves in place of the father's 'face'. For all its 'lighted windows', there is nothing to be seen in this summer sky; no one looks down through it, 'Not even my father'. The very transparency of the sunlit atmosphere is another form of 'blank obstruction'.

Once again, this Victorian daughter poet finds that the routes of vision, which might lead to the beloved dead, are blocked. Her imagination finds only the literal, spiritless spaces of the real sky, and remains 'alone, alone'. This moment in the garden is a crucial and symbolic one. 'June' is not just a time of year, but the sign of Aurora's poetic success. When Romney returns at the end of the poem to make a very different proposal of marriage, the memory of this day in June provides the *leitmotif* of his recognition of Aurora's superiority over himself. He greets her, for instance, as the 'same Aurora of the bright June-day' (VIII, 320), and as his unfailing 'June-day friend' (VIII, 609). June is the summer and high noon of her poetic ambition, and it is the June in her which proves, at the end, resilient and triumphant.

However, at the time, the June-day also has another connotation. Aurora finds that the cost of her ambition is not only the loss of Romney, but the loss, in her imagination, of the figure of her father. The windows of the 'June-heaven' are empty and its light is 'deaf'. The place where the daughter poet realises her vocation, and ambitiously crowns herself poet, is the place where she must also realise her desolation and her disinheritance. Aurora's imagination finds that the place, for all its sun and roses, is still, to her, a desert:

> Oh, alone, alone,—
> Not troubling any in heaven, nor any on earth,
> I stood there in the garden . . .

It is interesting that a little earlier, when Aurora crowns herself a poet with audacious but premature self-confidence, she crowns herself not with bay or myrtle, but with 'ivy' (II, 50); which is, she tells, 'as good to grow on graves/ As twist about a thyrsus' (II, 51–2). She chooses as the symbol of her new-found power, one that will remind her of 'graves'. The association lies at the heart of Barrett Browning's poetics. Although the sunny stage-set of Aurora's poetic triumph is a garden in June, the true landscape of her poetic consciousness is still that of 'a desert place' full of 'tombs'.

The extent to which the quest for the father in *Aurora Leigh* is also an intensely personal one is suggested by a passage in Book V, where Aurora admits she envies other poets, not their work, but their appreciative families. She therefore envies Mark Gage his mother, on whose knee he 'lays his last book's prodigal review' (V, 525). It is clearly Barrett Browning herself who speaks so feelingly here of the other poet's mother. Parents are still, in her imagination, the inspiration and the goal of writing, and it is in the knowledge of what she herself has lost that she then invokes their once powerful names:

> Dearest father,—mother sweet,—
> I speak the names out sometimes by myself,
> And make the silence shiver. They sound strange,
> As Hindostanee to an Ind-born man

Accustomed many years to English speech;
Or lovely poet-words grown obsolete,
Which will not leave off singing. Up in heaven
I have my father,—with my mother's face
Beside him in a blotch of heavenly light;
No more for earth's familiar, household use,
No more. The best verse written by this hand
Can never reach them where they sit, to seem
Well done to *them*.

(V, 540–52)

Just as once the 'prattling child' kept company with the 'silent' father, and just as the girl struggled for self-expression beside his 'stone-dead' body, so here the poet still tests her words, her 'lovely poet-words', against the fact of father's and mother's absence. But against that absence they ring false. 'They sound strange' and 'obsolete'. The names which serve at the start as an invocation of the daughter's beloved first muses become, for lack of any response, a mere poeticism—a tired routine. 'Dearest father,—mother sweet' is a nostalgic and redundant call. To go on invoking presences which do not reply, and which may not be attending any more, is to indulge in a mere incantation of sweet names. ' "O Muse, benignant Muse" ' is the rashly confident summons of the immature poet. The mature poet no longer calls, but stands alone in 'the melancholy desert'.

Once again, Aurora finds that the actual sky mocks her nostalgic imaginative aspirations. 'Up in heaven/ I have my father,' she thinks. But the religious and Romantic possibilities of that 'heaven' have also 'grown obsolete'. The best she can imagine is 'a blotch of heavenly light' where her mother's face might be. The larger visionary scope of skies is denied to this Victorian daughter, and in their place she confronts only the ordinary, empty atmosphere. Her imagination thus begins to learn its disinheritance even from 'the Dead'. These are increasingly distant and irrecoverable figures, who do not answer to their own dear names, and whose presences are gradually lost behind the bare literalness of the contemporary world.

The story of Aurora's development as a woman poet is thus one which depends on a characteristic poetics of the 'disinherited' daughter. But it also depends on a poetics of the 'disinherited' Victorian. The two are linked. Aurora finds, not only that the spirit of the one particular father is absent from the new landscapes of her life, but also that the spirit of the literary 'grandfathers' has gone. Even Italy, for all the erotic and maternal splendour of her hills, remains an alien and empty landscape which repudiates the mythopoeic yearnings of this belated poet. When Aurora approaches the Italian border, she needily invokes some sentient spirit of the place:

> My own hills! Are you 'ware of me, my hills,
> How I burn toward you? do you feel to-night
> The urgency and yearning of my soul,
> As sleeping mothers feel the sucking babe
> And smile?
>
> (V, 1266-71)

But she is too honest to grant her own wishes, and the answer she supplies is negative: 'Still ye go/ Your own determined, calm, indifferent way' (V, 1273-4). Her retrogressive desire for a mother, or at least for some mothering spirit of Nature, is denied, and she confronts a landscape which is merely 'determined, calm, indifferent'. Aurora must learn, even in Italy, to stand alone in the desert, and to write without mythologies and

132

without muses. Orphaned of both father and 'grand-fathers', this Victorian daughter stands alone in the literal, indifferent and unhaunted landscapes of the world, and finds in these desert plains the place of poetry.

However, it is not till nearly the end of *Aurora Leigh* that this literalism of the imagination is accepted without regret. When Aurora first reaches Italy, her thoughts are still moved by nostalgia for the past. She writes:

> And then I did not think, 'My Italy,'
> I thought 'My father!' O my father's house,
> Without his presence!
>
> (VII, 490–2)

Italy cannot yet make up for what Aurora has lost. The place is still, in her consciousness, only an outer shell of something that has fled: the father's 'presence'. It is that father who might have given significance to the place, like some presiding *genius loci*, or answering muse. But there is only the place, without its spirit; the house without the father in it.

The connection between the fact of fatherlessness and poetic creativity is made a few lines later, when Aurora moralises on the sense of loss which the beauty of Italy does not alleviate but merely reinforces. The idea of her father's empty house reminds her of the fate of being without dreams in an alien world. She writes:

> 'Tis only good to be or here or there,
> Because we had a dream on such a stone,
> Or this or that,—but, once being wholly waked
> And come back to the stone without the dream,
> We trip upon't,—alas, and hurt ourselves;
> Or else it falls on us and grinds us flat,

The heaviest gravestone on this burying earth.
(VII, 497–503)

To wake altogether from dreams, this Victorian poet declares, is to find the place forlorn and literal and full of graves. Without the spirit of things, the earth is a place which seems to kill the dreaming spirit of the poet with the weight of its gravestones. Yet, to *wake* from dreams has been the long and repeated experience of this 'orphaned' poet. She woke first to 'full life' beside her 'stone-dead father'. Later, she woke 'slowly, by degrees' from dreams of 'visionary chariots'. Now, she wakes again among 'stones' which, because of the failure of her father's 'presence', are all like gravestones. The 'burying earth' is the cruel but authentic landscape of her waking poetic consciousness.

Thus, in spite of her declared individualistic and Christian world-view, Barrett Browning's imagination is in fact shaped by a different and more pessimistic creed. That imagination rejects any mystical encounter with the dead, and it rejects any poetic mythologising of the landscape. Having lost the smile of her beloved father so absolutely, it is the absence of his spirit which characterises the world of the daughter. She must survive without dreams of him in the modern, urbane, materialistic age which is her own. Having been 'disinherited' of the father, she is 'disinherited' also of the past, and the world comes bare and literal to her imagination.

But the sense of graves remains strong in Aurora's consciousness, and they continue to underlie her new perceptions of Italy. 'My graves are calm,/ And do not too much hurt me' (VII, 929–30), she tells at one point, revealing how far 'graves' are something carried in the soul, as well as found in the landscape. A little later, she thinks she might be able to forget the dead altogether, and in a fine simile imagines how she might 'be a man' (VII, 985) and seal off the past from her consciousness:

> I'm not too much
> A woman, not to be a man for once
> And bury all my Dead like Alaric,
> Depositing the treasures of my soul
> In this drained watercourse, then letting flow
> The river of life again with commerce-ships
> And pleasure-barges full of silks and songs.
> (VII, 984–90).

metaphors

Nonetheless, the language works against the intentions of the speaker. However much she may bury them again, the 'Dead' are still 'the treasures' of her 'soul', and all the richest 'silks and songs' of the river of life are poor by comparison. Below this brilliant, commercial, busy world of 'silks and songs', the sense of 'graves' remains strong and seductive. All the other riches her imagination has gained continue to be measured against their preciousness, and in the end, the passage betrays the fact that this poet is still indeed 'too much/ A woman' to repress the dead so successfully. The high enterprise of her life and poetry, of her 'silks and songs', will retain this difference from that of men.

After this movingly reluctant attempt to bury the past, Aurora makes one last bid to find her father. The woman cannot yet relinquish what the man might bury with ease. In Florence, Aurora begins to discover her independence as a woman and her success as a poet, but she discovers them, at first, only in sad contrast to the past:

> How I heard
> My father's step on that deserted ground,

His voice along that silence, as he told
The names of bird and insect, tree and flower,
And all the presentations of the stars
Across Valdarno, interposing still
'My child,' 'my child.' When fathers say 'my child,'
'Tis easier to conceive the universe,
And life's transitions down the steps of law.

(VII, 1110–18)

This touchingly heartfelt memory of the father's authoritative presence in childhood is one which connects that presence with the child's whole conception of 'the universe'. It is the father who gives, not only the 'names' of things, like Adam in the garden, but the meaning of things as well: 'the steps of law'. However, the woman is no longer a child, and the father is no longer there, to be her authority and her guide. To have power to walk alone and to be one's own namer of the world is to have lost for certain that first dependent companionship in the Eden of childhood. As a result, the woman who has become a namer and a poet in her own right walks on a 'deserted ground'. Even Valdarno, with all its birds and flowers and stars, seems, in the daughter's 'orphaned' consciousness, but a desert plain. In such a place she must 'conceive the universe' alone.

Aurora's life in Italy is thus one of gradually learned resignation and independence. It is not the realisation that she has loved and lost Romney, but that she has loved and lost her father, which tests and educates her imagination. It is this loss which turns the landscapes even of Italy into a 'melancholy desert'. She then makes one last attempt to break this mental solitude when she returns to visit the house in which she lived alone with him, as a child. The episode marks the last stage of Barrett Browning's long, hard quest for her beloved first muse. 'I rode once to the little mountain-house/ As fast

as if to find my father there' (VII, 1119–20), she writes.
What Aurora finds, however, is something else:

> The house's front
> Was cased with lingots of ripe Indian corn
> In tessellated order and device
> Of golden patterns, not a stone of wall
> Uncovered,—not an inch of room to grow
> A vine-leaf.
>
> (VII, 1123–8)

Not only is the place barely recognisable, but Aurora is
forced to witness the actual destruction of her father's
bowers of vines: 'the lads were busy with their staves/ In
shout and laughter, stripping every bough/ As bare as
winter' (VII, 1135–7). This is reminiscent of
Wordsworth's 'Nutting', and by implication of Barrett
Browning's early quest poems, which went in search of
'a spirit in the woods'. But if it is this old hope which
drives Aurora back to the landscape of her childhood, the
reality which confronts her is very different, and her
reaction is a sign of it: 'Enough. My horse recoiled before
my heart;/ I turned the rein abruptly' (VII, 1140–1).

The horror of this literal devastation of the father's
garden is unmistakable. To interpret the episode as an
ideological statement about the patriarchal house being
taken over by 'female fertility symbols',[12] as Sandra
Gilbert does, is to miss the emotional point. Aurora is
appalled and stunned by what she sees. But she is also
harshly educated by it. The father's absence is finally
experienced for what it is: the total failure of an old,
idyllic world of childhood and of natural abundance and
of Romantic hauntings. The bower has been lost, the
garden deserted, all over again, and in their place Aurora
finds the crudely utilitarian rule of trade and wealth: the
'tessellated order and device/ Of golden patterns'.

The episode not only signifies at last the daughter's complete 'disinheritance' by the past; it also expresses something of the nature of the present in which she must live and write. The garden was always a place of lost childhood gladness in Barrett Browning's early poems. But in *Aurora Leigh* this loss has a new point. Aurora's nostalgic expedition to 'the little mountain-house' turns into a necessary confrontation with the remorseless order of the contemporary world. Aurora finds, not the ghostly spirits of the past, but the 'real everyday life of our age'. The father's Romantic garden has been ruined and overrun by a new order of things. The implication, not only of this one passage but of the whole poem, is that the new order is Barrett Browning's own. The pain of Aurora's discovery is the pain of the poet in her, at meeting 'face to face & without mask the Humanity of the age'. That this 'Humanity' is discovered at the expense of her beloved father's face is something the poem has predicted from its very first lines.

This episode represents the end of the quest. After the journey to her father's house, Aurora is resigned to be alone. She writes:

> That was trial enough
> Of graves. I would not visit, if I could,
> My father's, or my mother's any more . . .
> (VII, 1142–4)

The whole poem has been, till now, a 'trial' of 'graves'. Aurora has carried the sense of them, and the sense of one in particular, in her soul and in her imagination's eye. Those 'graves' came to mark and underlie the landscapes of the whole world. Whether the place was England or Italy, it was, to the 'orphaned' daughter, a burial ground, a place of stones, a desert plain.

138

However, after the expedition to the father's house, Aurora is changed. She is no longer nostalgic, lonely and haunted. She no longer searches out the spirits of her childhood's past, or calls the names of her 'Dearest father,—mother sweet'. Instead, she is content with the present. In the state of sudden creative exhilaration which ensues, the world around her acquires a new sufficiency and brilliance. She declares:

> I'm happy. It's sublime,
> This perfect solitude of foreign lands!
> To be, as if you had not been till then,
> And were then, simply that you chose to be . . .
> . . . possess, yourself,
> A new world all alive with creatures new,
> New sun, new moon, new flowers, new people—ah,
> And be possessed by none of them!
>
> (VII, 1193–6, 1200–3)

Here, Aurora greets a world which is no longer a substitute for her father's face and her father's presence. For the first time, her loneliness does not stem from a sense of his lack and absence, but is a 'perfect solitude', desired and willed. This is not the 'solitude' of the desert, in which objects seemed to be only more burial-stones on her consciousness; it is the 'solitude of foreign lands' that are full of new, live, ordinary things: 'New sun, new moon, new flowers, new people'. No longer 'possessed' by the figure of the absent father, Aurora gains a whole world for poetry instead, and gains it, suddenly, for free. There is no exchange in this acceptance of a 'new world all alive'. The last journey to the father's devastated garden, for all its horror, finally releases her from the burden of the past, and from the burden of her disinheritance. Self-sufficient and self-possessed, she at last knows her emancipation, as a woman and as a poet, from the long shadow of the father muse.

Aurora Leigh thus maps, in its sub-plot, the progress of Barrett Browning's own last quest for the father, whose silence in real life she was to hear in her imagination for so many years after she had 'disinherited' herself in actuality from his affection. Throughout the poem she registers that silence, she appeals against it and even hopes to break it, until, finally, she dispossesses herself of the memory of it in a 'new world all alive with creatures new'. In the end, the daughter poet who has been 'orphaned' and 'disinherited', both in her life and in her poetic consciousness, realises that she has also therefore been freed—freed to make her loss and her loneliness creative. It is over the daughter's failed quest for the absent father that the other quest of the poem—the quest for a sister—can proceed.

Chapter Seven

' "Come with me, sweetest sister" ': The Poet's Last Quest

Nay, if there's room for poets in this world
A little overgrown (I think there is),
Their sole work is to represent the age,
Their age, not Charlemagne's,—this live, throbbing age,
That brawls, cheats, maddens, calculates, aspires,
And spends more passion, more heroic heat,
Betwixt the mirrors of its drawing-rooms,
Than Roland with his knights at Roncesvalles.

(V, 200-7)

In *Aurora Leigh* Barrett Browning superimposes on the imagination's private quest and elegy for the dead, a public manifesto for poetry. Poets, she declares, must reject the past, and embrace instead the unglamorous domestic realities of the age. This message of commitment to the contemporary world is one which she promulgates with enthusiasm, but which is not fulfilled in practice until Aurora rejects her own personal past, and embraces the loneliness of her 'orphaned' state. Thus the theory of imaginative contemporaneity, which

141

is Barrett Browning's distinctive and powerful poetic creed, is linked to Aurora's eventual rejection of the quest for her dead father. The woman's poetic theory is tested on the pulses of the daughter. It is only by being dispossessed of the imagination's sense of 'the Dead' that this woman poet finally succeeds in realising her own poetics of contemporary commitment. The landscapes of *Aurora Leigh* are those which were feared and predicted in *Casa Guidi Windows*. They are the bare and ordinary 'plains' of the present, from where it is no longer possible to 'look back to the hills behind'.

In *Aurora Leigh*, Barrett Browning thus rejects the temptation to retreat into a more heroic past, and repeatedly declares her intention to search the spirit of the age at its most secular and urbane. Perhaps the very seclusion of her adult life before marriage made her appreciate the age and the world outside all the more vividly. 'Denial of access to the Real made it fascinating to women,'[1] writes Ellen Moers. Once free in the real world of travel and political conflict, Barrett Browning's imagination had to make up for long years of deprivation. Yet, as early as 1845 she had stated her poetic principles to Robert, with touching optimism, from her invalid's seclusion: 'Let us all aspire rather to *Life* . . . For there is poetry *everywhere*' (*Letters: 1845–1846*, I, 43). *Aurora Leigh* is the witness of how far that '*everywhere*' was to be enlarged for her during the next ten years.

Aurora Leigh does not succeed in being a consistently great poem, but it does succeed in being a new kind of poem, and of communicating the message of its newness. The passionate, garrulous, hectoring, inspired Aurora discourses on the world before her with the conviction of an imaginative discovery. It is this sense of mission towards the times which probably inspired the enthusiasm with which the work was received, particularly by other writers and poets. George Eliot read it at least three times, and wrote of her strong 'sense of communion'[2] with the author. Swinburne, Leigh Hunt, Landor, Ruskin, Robert Lytton and Dante Gabriel Rossetti all praised it generously, and stinted no comparison with the works of the greatest poets.[3] It seems that *Aurora Leigh* offered a theory and practice of imaginative contemporariness which precisely answered the needs of the age.

However, the poem confronts the contemporary world, 'this live, throbbing age', from the express point of view of a woman. This bias is overt and stressed. As a result, the work is one of the most outspoken pieces of 'feminist' imaginative writing in the mid-nineteenth century. Barrett Browning was delighted to hear of the small scandals it provoked: that a lady of sixty, for instance, felt morally corrupted by it, and that the 'mammas of England'[4] had forbidden their daughters to read it. In fact, she exaggerates the public outcry which greeted the work's publication; but her pleasure in stirring up a scandal is evident. In one of her letters she assesses the reasons for this public disapprobation:

> What has given most offence in the book, more than the story of Marian—far more!—has been the reference to the condition of women in our cities, which a woman oughtn't to refer to, by any manner of means, says the conventional tradition. Now I have thought deeply otherwise. If a woman ignores these wrongs, then may women as a sex continue to suffer them; there is no help for any of us—let us be dumb and die. (*Kenyon*, II, 254)

In fact, there are few outspoken references to 'the condition of women in our cities' in *Aurora Leigh*, and those few *are* connected with 'the story of Marian', who is tricked into a brothel where she is drugged and raped.

It is she who provides the link with the other 'women in our cities', and who justifies the author's intention to refer to them.

However, the real 'feminist' provocation of *Aurora Leigh* is not the fact of an occasional chance reference to prostitution, but the attitude of the speaker towards the subject. In Book VI, Marian Erle's description of her experience in the brothel ends by exactly paralleling the point in the letter. She declares:

> 'Enough so!—it is plain enough so. True,
> We wretches cannot tell out all our wrong
> Without offence to decent happy folk.
> I know that we must scrupulously hint
> With half-words, delicate reserves, the thing
> Which no one scrupled we should feel in full.'
>
> (VI, 1219–24)

Instead of apologising for what she must say, Marian turns the accusation against those who forbid a woman to mention these things. She forcefully refuses to court either sympathy or forgiveness, and instead lays the blame at the feet of 'decent happy folk' who are nice with words, but are unaffronted by the facts. It is this declared intention to break the verbal taboos of the age which characterises Barrett Browning's references to prostitution, and which probably gave offence to the Victorian public. The triple female speaker of this poem—Barrett Browning, Aurora and Marian—is a sure and unsubtle ruse by which to break 'the conventional tradition' that 'a woman oughtn't to refer to' these things.

Barrett Browning's portrayal of Marian Erle is to some extent indebted to Mrs Gaskell's *Ruth*, which she read in 1853, and of which she wrote enthusiastically and complicitously to its author: 'I am grateful to you as a woman for having so treated such a subject'.[5] But Barrett Browning's own treatment of the 'subject' of the fallen woman differs significantly from her predecessor's. Unlike Mrs Gaskell, she is not concerned to gain a Christian forgiveness for her heroine, but rather to expose the absurdity of a culture in which virtue is an affair of words, not deeds. It is the conspiracy of silence among the 'decent happy folk', especially among the women, which she would break by writing. Such silence permits the very evils which it will not name, and thus is ultimately responsible, as Lady Waldemar is believed responsible in the story, for the sexual exploitation of other women. 'If a woman ignores these wrongs, then may women as a sex continue to suffer them,' Barrett Browning declared. Her responsibility as a poet is towards those other women whom silence has victimised. Marian's experience of being drugged and raped is one which the age refuses to hear, and especially refuses to hear from the lips of a woman. Not only, therefore, does Barrett Browning provocatively assume the moral and political right to speak, but she also accuses the guardians of decency and delicacy of being themselves corrupt. To be 'dumb', she claims, is to assent to suffering. If women in particular are 'dumb', as men would have them, they assent to their own suffering as a sex. The political motive of simply speaking out, of refusing to 'be dumb and die', is one which, in *Aurora Leigh*, Barrett Browning outrageously flaunts.

This subversive attitude to the codes of verbal propriety enforced on women is evident in much of Barrett Browning's work. In 1861, the year of her death, she submitted a poem, 'Lord Walter's Wife', to the *Cornhill Magazine*, which was then edited by Thackeray. To her surprise—but also to her glee—it was rejected for being morally unsuitable. 'Thackeray has turned me out of the "Cornhill" for indecency' (*Kenyon*, II, 443), she reported, with barely disguised pride. The poem criticises that attitude of men which claims the prerogative to flirt, even with a married woman, but is quick to condemn the very same woman if she responds. It is not only the double standard which is under attack, but also the insulting assumption that the woman's role is to listen in passive and unreciprocating silence to the man's amorous declarations. ' "You take us for harlots, I tell you, and not for the women we are",'[6] Lord Walters's wife responds indignantly.

To Thackeray himself, Barrett Browning wrote a forceful vindication of her intentions in the poem:

> I don't like coarse subjects, or the coarse treatment of any subject. But I am deeply convinced that the corruption of our society requires not shut doors and windows, but light and air: and that it is exactly because pure and prosperous women choose to *ignore* vice, that miserable women suffer wrong by it everywhere. Has paterfamilias, with his Oriental traditions and veiled female faces, very successfully dealt with a certain class of evil? What if materfamilias, with her quick sure instincts and honest innocent eyes, do more towards their expulsion by simply looking at them and calling them by their names? (*Kenyon*, II, 445)

The passage reveals how quickly the Victorian mind moves from the idea of a mildly adulterous flirtation to the idea of the fallen woman. Barrett Browning has written a poem about flirtation, but she defends it as if it were about prostitution. Her language then seems to tread a very fine line between moral condemnation and political justification. The 'pure', her language tells, are likely to be also the 'prosperous', while 'vice' is something by which 'miserable women suffer wrong'.

She keeps a strong moral perspective while subtly implying not only that 'vice' is an oppression laid upon the poor, but that it is also the direct result of the chosen ignorance of the 'pure and prosperous'. The blame returns to the door of sheltered, wealthy women.

But it also returns against men. The simile of the harem is a powerful and wrathful one. The fathers' way of dealing with these things is to keep the women hushed and veiled, and thus, from enforced sexual modesty, impotent to change the system in which they too are trapped. The modesty of the wives of 'paterfamilias' is a blindfold which forbids them to see their own situation as well. It is time, Barrett Browning claims, that women took off their veils and used their eyes. By 'simply looking at them and calling them by their names', women might rid society of the vices of which they are all victims. This statement is characteristic in that it does not range Madonnas against Magdalens, pure women against fallen women; it ranges them all against men, against 'paterfamilias'. Whether veiled or unveiled, women's lot is that of the harem. Both the exaggerated modesty of the 'pure and prosperous' and the exploited immodesty of the 'miserable' serve to perpetuate the sexual rule of men.

It is this radical liaison between women, who are united in the purpose of speaking out, which characterises *Aurora Leigh*. It is true, as Cora Kaplan writes, that Marian Erle's 'embourgoisement in terms of language and understanding occurs at embarrassing speed.'[7] The characterisation of *Aurora Leigh* is, indeed, often extremist and unconvincing. However, in some ways the figure of Marian represents a significant advance in the literature of the fallen woman. While Hester Prynne, Hetty Sorrel and Ruth are all to some extent made an exception, and 'pardoned for sexual activity' because they 'love',[8] Marian is simply raped in a brothel. She is thus linked with the other unmentionable women who, for whatever reason, have also been tricked into a brothel. The fact of the rape makes Marian, not an individual exception to the rule of vice, but an example for a general cause. She is only one of the 'miserable women' who 'suffer wrong . . . everywhere'. Barrett Browning then contests the whole Victorian myth of contamination by bringing Marian out of the brothel to live with her unsullied heroine,[9] not because Aurora must learn Christian charity, but because, as a woman, she must write about such things. The relation between Aurora and Marian constitutes an ideological league of women defying, both in practice and in word, the divisions of their society.

Marian's description of her rape may be in one sense an improbably articulate account. But in another sense that very confidence of speech makes a powerful political point. Instead of retiring into a self-effacing and thus conventionally innocent silence, she accuses the world around her, which is so vociferous to condemn but not to cure. When asked by Aurora how she came by her child, Marian answers impatiently:

> 'I found him where
> I found my curse,—in the gutter, with my shame!
> What have you, any of you, to say to that,
> Who all are happy, and sit safe and high,
> And never spoke before to arraign my right
> To grief itself? What, what, . . . being beaten down
> By hoofs of maddened oxen into a ditch,
> Half-dead, whole mangled, when a girl at last
> Breathes, sees . . . and finds there, bedded in her flesh
> Because of the extremity of the shock,
> Some coin of price!
>   . . .

You all put up your finger—"See the thief!
"Observe what precious thing she has come to filch.
"How bad those girls are!" '

(VI, 671–81, 685–7)

The issue here is not whether the fallen woman is guilty, but whether those who ' "never spoke before" ' are guilty. Marian attacks the hypocritical readiness of society to condemn what it is too modest to speak about.

The link between sexual innocence and silence is one which Barrett Browning is keen to break in every way, and Marian's otherwise unconvincing rise to the middle class is one of the tactics she uses. While Hester Prynne weaves a strange half-guilty, half-liberating meaning round the letter 'A', and Hetty Sorrel remains helpless and inarticulate, and Ruth keeps to an unassertive and saintly quietude, Marian speaks strongly in her own defence. She thus breaks the intriguing enigma that surrounds the figure of the fallen woman, and breaks the ideological association, so often used to justify her in Victorian literature, between innocence and silence. Such silence, Barrett Browning claims, is merely an excuse for the system of 'paterfamilias' to continue. It is an excuse to keep women confined in the condition either of the harem or the brothel.

The principle of speaking, then, which Barrett Browning asserts so confidently and magnanimously in the *Sonnets from the Portuguese*, becomes, in *Aurora Leigh*, a principle of political and sexual defiance. It has as its starting point the fact that women are supposed to ' "sit safe and high" '. She defies this convention, not by any very clear-sighted or informed depiction of prostitution, but simply by her declared intention to write about it. Silence, for this poet, is not a sign of innocence but a sign of guilt. Thus, although she has no very strong understanding of her working-class heroine as a

149

character, she has a very strong sense of how, being the subject of speech is itself a subversion of the rules. Even Marian is not just a mute and helpless object. The notorious and defiant characteristic of this poem—'one of the longest poems in the world'[10] according to Swinburne—is that its three female speakers—Barrett Browning, Aurora and Marian—will *not* 'be dumb and die'.

Just how much the Victorian myth of contamination was a verbal myth is shown by the critics' reaction to *Ruth*. ' "An unfit subject for fiction" is *the* thing to say about it,'[11] Mrs Gaskell wrote ruefully. The unfitness was of course not literary, but moral. The subject of the fallen woman was one that might sully the author. As shown by that critic who deplored Mrs Gaskell's 'loss of reputation',[12] the sexual slur falls on the woman who dares to speak or write. All Mrs Gaskell's protestations about Ruth's heavenly purity could not appease this moral censoriousness. In fact, Barrett Browning reproached Mrs Gaskell for having Ruth die at the end,[13] and in her own variant of the story rejects any hint of expiation. Marian not only condemns the hypocrisy of the world; she also refuses to accept the world's version of respectability. Romney's offer of marriage and legalised paternity has no attraction for her. She rejects the social authority of the father's name with indignation: 'We only never call him fatherless/ Who has God and his mother' (IX, 414–15). This narrative tactic to free Romney for Aurora, however emotionally unconvincing, makes an ideological point which is in keeping with Barrett Browning's purpose. Not only is Marian innocent, but she proves that innocence by having the confidence to live and speak in her own right. That confidence is the real ideological victory of *Aurora Leigh*.

However, the role of Marian is not only that of the

vindicated fallen woman. Although Marian tells her own story, with challenging moral assurance, it is Aurora who writes it. The relationship between them thus reflects on Aurora's purpose as a poet. Not only does she take up with the other woman, and without the man for whom they should be rivals; she also takes up Marian's story as her own. That the story is a forbidden one throws into relief Aurora's consciousness of being a woman poet whose purpose is to break the rule of silence. In Marian she finds a subject which the world denies and which convention prohibits her from telling. She tells it, therefore, with crusading energy:

> all my soul rose up to take her part
> Against the world's successes, virtues, fames.
> 'Come with me, sweetest sister,' I returned . . .
> (VII, 115–17)

Aurora's imagination finds in Marian the unpermitted story of the age, and she embraces it with zeal. As Dolores Rosenblum writes: 'The finding of Marian confirms Aurora's previous discovery of a living poetics',[14] and thus justifies her new mission to express 'this live, throbbing age' in art. Marian is the object of Aurora's quest to tell.

This quest is described in Book VI. Aurora has a glimpse of Marian's face in the Paris streets and immediately sets out to find her. But the urgency with which she pursues her object suggests a need which goes beyond the requirements of the plot. It is not only concern for her lost sister which drives Aurora; it is an obsession to find at least one face that is not, like all the others, absent or dead. The pursuit through the Paris streets parallels another journey in Aurora's consciousness that takes her back through her old guilty intimations of mortality. It is as if her imagination cannot, at first, trust this quest to be different.

Aurora's first sight of Marian's face occurs just after she has made one of her declarations of poetic principle. She disparages those poets who stay tethered to the worn poeticisms of 'lily' and 'rose' (VI, 184), and declares that there is more real poetry in 'the hungry beggar-boy' (VI, 186) who has been foolishly scorned 'for a flower or two' (VI, 192). Barrett Browning advocates not only that poetry should be contemporary, but also that it should be humanised. It is at this point in the poem that she glimpses Marian's face among the crowds. Marian appears like the muse of Aurora's new, different, contemporary poetics. She is not exactly the 'beggar-boy', but his female equivalent.

However, the poet's imagination is not yet educated in the contemporaneity she advocates in theory. Immediately, Marian's living face blurs with the memory of others. Above all it is confused, as Alethea Hayter[15] points out, with the memory of Bro's. Aurora imagines it surfacing like the face of the dead:

> When something floats up suddenly, out there,
> Turns over . . . a dead face, known once alive . . .
> So old, so new!
>
> (VI, 238–40)

This confusion of the 'old' and the 'new' suggests how far back Barrett Browning's imagination has travelled. Marian brings to the surface of consciousness the idea of a face which the poet never dared imagine before. She writes:

> That face persists,
> It floats up, it turns over in my mind,
> As like to Marian as one dead is like
> The same alive.
>
> (VI, 308–11)

This confusion between the dead and the living—
between, as it were, the dead brother and the living
sister—shows how far the figure of Marian is still only a
substitute for the old forsaking muses. Her face appears
like all the faces that the June sky or the bitter sea have
separated from the surviving woman poet.

This association is stressed by Aurora's strange,
panicky and pessimistic reaction to Marian's disappear-
ance among the crowds:

> No Marian; nowhere Marian. Almost, now,
> I could call Marian, Marian, with the shriek
> Of desperate creatures calling for the Dead.
> (VI, 255-7)

There is no narrative logic to this sudden and persistent
association of Marian with 'the Dead'. It is entirely a
product of Barrett Browning's own experiences and
imaginative needs. Once again, *Aurora Leigh* conveys two
parallel stories. There is the story of the narrative,
which is one of literal economic and emotional survival
for the woman poet. But there is also the story of her
imaginative quests, which shows her much less certain
of that independence which really means disinheritance
from her past. Marian's tantalising evasion of Aurora in
Paris finds its meaning in the sub-text of Aurora's
repeatedly 'orphaned' consciousness.

However, the quest for Marian is ultimately different.
Unable to sleep, Aurora goes one day at dawn to the
flower market, and there finds the object of her search.
Once found, Marian is grasped with violent possessiveness:

> 'Marian, Marian!'—face to face—
> 'Marian! I find you. Shall I let you go?'

153

I held her two slight wrists with both my hands;
'Ah Marian, Marian, can I let you go?'
—She fluttered from me like a cyclamen,
As white, which taken in a sudden wind
Beats on against the palisade.—'Let pass',
She said at last. 'I will not,' I replied;
'I lost my sister Marian many days,
And sought her ever in my walks and prayers,
And, now I find her . . .

(VI, 441–51)

Whereas the old quests for father and mother had to fail, because the daughter lives and writes only by being 'orphaned' of the father's law and of the mother's womanliness, the quest for a sister succeeds. She is the muse of this woman poet's contemporaneity and commitment. This is the end of Aurora's many days' search, but it is also the end of Barrett Browning's many years' search for the object that will serve for a new, vitally contemporary woman's poetry. ' "I lost my sister Marian many days . . . And, now I find her." '

Critics have described the figure of Marian as, for instance, that of a 'mother-muse',[16] which Aurora must reject, as 'a symbol for the birth of [Aurora's] self',[17] and as a figure for the living truth which 'echoes and reinforces the truth Aurora claims for herself.'[18] But Marian is also, emphatically, a sister, and the often repeated term carries a nearly modern connotation of a liaison against the rules. Aurora does not find a real sister; she makes a sister of the lost other woman. The moral and political intrepidity of this act is part of the point, not only of Aurora's story, but also of Barrett Browning's new poetics. These are no longer a poetics of the daughter, but of the woman; and of a woman conscious of her imagination's responsibility towards her sex: 'it is exactly because pure and prosperous

154

women choose to *ignore* vice, that miserable women suffer wrong by it everywhere.' Aurora seeks out Marian with the urgency, not only of a poet seeking her last muse, but of a woman making political amends for the oppression of her sex. Aurora does, in fact, succeed where Romney, the philanthropist, fails. Her imagination marries with the other, fallen woman, and does so with much more conviction and desire.' "Come with me, sweetest sister," I returned.'

Once found, Aurora follows her sister Marian home with the dogged pertinacity of one for whom it has become a matter of life and death:

> Then she led
> The way, and I, as by a narrow plank
> Across devouring waters, followed her,
> Stepping by her footsteps, breathing by her breath,
> And holding her with eyes that would not slip . . .
> (VI, 500–4)

It is interesting that, although Aurora takes the philanthropist Romney's place in her relation to Marian, it is really Marian who finally saves *her*. 'The way' she takes leads significantly over the 'devouring waters', as if to say, that only by holding firm to this new sister of the present will Aurora escape the past's overwhelming message of grief. The quest for Marian is a quest to go on living and writing, in spite of and even, now, careless of, the seductive, haunting memories of the dead. The 'disinherited' Victorian daughter has become a woman and a poet in her own right, and the figure of Marian is the muse of her new direction and purpose on the imagination's desert plains.

Thus *Aurora Leigh* is the culmination of Barrett Browning's lifelong search for a poetics which will express her imaginative intentions as a Victorian and as a woman. Her ambition to be faithful to the 'age' and to find 'poetry *everywhere*' is realised in this epic which goes 'rushing into drawing-rooms and the like'. Its contemporaneity is achieved, however, through a hard, slow but total dispossession of the father. Aurora's progress towards a political and imaginative commitment to the age is a progress over graves. The sense of the father's inevitable and necessary death was always, from her earliest poems, the condition of Barrett Browning's bid for poetic power. But in *Aurora Leigh* that death is realised as an imaginative disinheritance which finds the father, not only lost, but also irrelevant. The fear expressed in *Casa Guidi Windows* of being 'orphaned' and 'disinherited' *even* of 'the Dead' is a fear which *Aurora Leigh* brilliantly and unsparingly realises.

However, in doing so it permits the fulfilment of a different quest. Marian Erle, the unmentionable, fallen other woman of Victorian society is the object of this quest and the muse of this 'unscrupulously epic' poem. While all Barrett Browning's earlier figures for the muse —her father, mother, brother, and even lover—remain absent and unanswering in her poems, Marian answers Aurora's 'desperate' call, and alone returns from the regions of 'the Dead' to make the desert place bearable. She *is* the answer to Barrett Browning's call for a new, contemporary, transgressive woman's poetry which will not 'be dumb and die'.

Meanwhile, such poetry has been written. 'I'm a woman, sir' (VIII, 1130), Aurora a little impatiently reminds Romney at the end. This 'epic of the literary woman',[19] which has also been grandly called a 'feminist hymn',[20] insists from beginning to end on the fact of its female authorship. 'I write', Aurora announces at the beginning, and at the end she once more reminds the reader that this is the story of writing as well as of loving: 'I have written day by day' (IX, 725).

Not only does *Aurora Leigh* connect with fine insouciance the high and the low, the epic and the domestic, the poetic and the banal; it also connects the writing of poetry with the cause of the silenced woman. The presiding muse of this woman's poem is precisely that outlawed figure of the sexually fallen woman, who, jointly with her sister poet, dares nonetheless to speak. 'I'm a woman, sir' is a statement made on behalf of all women, whether fallen or unfallen, working-class or middle-class, illegitimately mothers or illegitimately poets. It is this shared, confrontational, emancipatory right to language which marks Barrett Browning's sense of herself, at the height of her powers, as a woman poet, and as a poet speaking for women.

Notes

Chapter 1

1. *Athenaeum*, 1 June 1850, p.585.
2. Virginia Woolf, ' "Aurora Leigh" ', in *The Common Reader*, 2nd series (London, The Hogarth Press, 1932), p.208.
3. Ibid., p.202.
4. See Gardner B. Taplin, *The Life of Elizabeth Barrett Browning* (London, John Murray, 1957), p.407.
5. Hugh Walker, *The Literature of the Victorian Era* (1910; Cambridge, Cambridge University Press, 1921), p.368.
6. Oliver Elton, *The Brownings* (London, Edward Arnold, 1924), p.85.
7. Osbert Burdett, *The Brownings* (London, Constable, 1928), p.259.
8. G.K. Chesterton, *Robert Browning* (London, Macmillan, 1903), p.57.
9. Elton, op. cit., p.90.
10. Burdett, op. cit., p.16.
11. Lilian Whiting, *A Study of Elizabeth Barrett Browning* (London, 1899), p.168.
12. Ibid., pp.25-6.
13. Eric S. Robertson, *English Poetesses: A Series of Critical*

Biographies with Illustrative Extracts (London, 1883), prefatory note.

14. Ibid., p.xv.
15. Ibid., p.xiv.
16. *The Brontës: Their Lives, Friendships and Correspondence*, ed. Thomas James Wise and John Alexander Symington (1933; 4 vols, Oxford, Basil Blackwell, 1980), I, 155 (March 1837).
17. Elizabeth Barrett Browning, *Aurora Leigh*, intro. Cora Kaplan (London, The Women's Press, 1983).
18. John Stuart Mill, *The Subjection of Women* (London, Dent, Everyman's Library, 1929), pp.219–317, p.259.
19. *The Brontës: Their Lives, Friendships and Correspondence*, I, 11 (16 August 1849).
20. Elaine Showalter, 'Towards a Feminist Poetics', in *Women Writing and Writing about Women*, ed. Mary Jacobus (London, Croom Helm, 1979), p.35.
21. Cora Kaplan, Introduction to *Aurora Leigh* (London, The Women's Press, 1983), p.10.
22. See Taplin, op. cit., p.338.
23. G.H. Lewes, 'The Lady Novelists', in *The Westminster Review*, n.s. 2(1852), 129–41, p.129.
24. Mill, op. cit., p.287.
25. Elizabeth Barrett Browning, 'The Book of the Poets', in *The Complete Works of Elizabeth Barrett Browning*, ed. Charlotte Porter and Helen A. Clarke (6 vols, New York, Thomas Y. Crowell, 1900), VI, 304.
26. Ibid., VI, 251.
27. Mary Jacobus, 'Is There a Woman in This Text?' *New Literary History*, 14 (1982), 117–41, p.138.
28. Simone de Beauvoir, *The Second Sex*, trans. and ed. H.M. Parshley (1949; Harmondsworth, Penguin Books, 1972), p.29.
29. Ibid., p.16.
30. Jacques Lacan, 'God and the *Jouissance* of the Woman', in *Feminine Sexuality*, ed. Juliet Mitchell and Jacqueline Rose (London, Macmillan, 1982), p.141.
31. Maud Ellmann, 'Blanche', in *Criticism and Critical Theory*, ed. Jeremy Hawthorne (London, Edward Arnold, 1984), p.100.
32. Jacques Lacan, *Écrits*, trans. Alan Sheridan (London,

Tavistock Publications, 1977), p.67.

33. Jacques Lacan, 'A Love Letter', in *Feminine Sexuality*, p.151.

34. Jacqueline Rose, 'Introduction II', to *Feminine Sexuality*, p.50.

35. Ibid., p.54.

36. Luce Irigaray, 'When Our Lips Speak Together', trans. Carolyn Burke, *Signs*, 6 (1980), 69–79, p.77.

37. Hélène Cixous, 'Castration or Decapitation?' trans. Annette Kuhn, *Signs*, 7 (1981), 41–55, p.53.

38. Julia Kristeva, 'Oscillation between power and denial', an interview, trans. Marilyn A. August, in *New French Feminisms: An Anthology*, ed. Elaine Marks and Isabelle de Courtivron (Amherst, Mass., The University of Massachusetts Press, 1980), p.166.

39. Luce Irigaray, 'Women's Exile', interview with Luce Irigaray, *Ideology & Consciousness*, I (1977), 62–76, p.70.

40. Jacques Derrida, *Spurs: Nietzsche's Styles*, trans. Barbara Harlow (Chicago and London,The University of Chicago Press, 1979), p.37.

41. Ibid., p.49.

42. Ibid., p.41.

43. Mary Jacobus, 'Is There a Woman in This Text?' p.118.

44. Elizabeth L. Berg, 'The Third Woman', *Diacritics*, 12 (Summer 1982), 11–20, p.17.

45. Plato, *Ion*, in *The Dialogues of Plato*, trans. B. Jowett (4 vols, Oxford, Clarendon Press, 1953), I, 103–117, p.107.

46. Sigmund Freud, *Totem and Taboo*, in *The Standard Edition of the Complete Psychological Works of Sigmund Freud*, ed. James Strachey (24 vols, London, The Hogarth Press, 1966–74), XIII, 1–161, p.156.

47. Harold Bloom, *The Anxiety of Influence: A Theory of Poetry* (London, Oxford Univeristy Press, 1973), p.63.

48. See, for instance, Joanne Feit Diehl, ' "Come Slowly— Eden": An Exploration of Women Poets and Their Muse', *Signs*, 3 (1978), 572–87; Sandra M. Gilbert and Susan Gubar, *The Madwoman in the Attic: The Woman Writer and the Nineteenth-Century Literary Imagination* (New Haven and London, Yale University Press, 1979); Annette Kolodny, 'A Map for Rereading: Or, Gender and the Interpretation of Literary Texts', *New Literary History*, 3 (1980), 451–67.

49. Bloom, op. cit., p.94.

50. Mary Wollstonecraft, *A Vindication of the Rights of Woman*, ed.

Carol H. Poston (New York, W.W. Norton, 1975), p.43.

51. Robert Graves, *The White Goddess: A historical grammar of poetic myth*, enlarged edn (London, Faber, 1961), p.446.
52. Ibid., p.447.
53. Gilbert and Gubar, op. cit., p.47.
54. Margaret Homans, *Women Writers and Poetic Identity: Dorothy Wordsworth, Emily Brontë, and Emily Dickinson* (Princeton, N.J., Princeton University Press, 1980), p.39.

Chapter 2

1. Elizabeth Barrett Browning, 'To My Father on His Birthday', in *Complete Works*, 1, 100–1.
2. Virginia Woolf, *Three Guineas* (1938; Harmondsworth, Penguin Books, 1977), p.149.
3. Dorothy Hewlett, *Elizabeth Barrett Browning: A Life* (1952; New York, Octagon Books, 1972), p.47.
4. Gardner B. Taplin, *The Life of Elizabeth Barrett Browning* (London, John Murray, 1957), p.19.
5. Elaine Showalter, *A Literature of Their Own: British Women Novelists from Brontë to Lessing* (London, Virago, 1978), p.61.
6. Simone de Beauvoir, *The Second Sex* (1949; Harmondsworth, Penguin Books, 1972), p.314.
7. Ellen Moers, *Literary Women* (London, The Women's Press, 1978), pp.173–210.
8. See Madelyn Gutwirth, *Madame de Staël, Novelist: The Emergence of the Artist as Woman* (Urbana, Chicago and London, University of Illinois Press, 1978), p.43.
9. Ibid., p.42.
10. Madame de Staël, *Corinne ou L'Italie* (Paris, 1845), p.13.
11. Ibid., p.259.
12. Michael Meredith, 'The Wounded Heroine: Elizabeth Barrett's Sophocles', *Studies in Browning and His Circle*, 3 (1975), 1–12, p.8.
13. *The George Eliot Letters*, ed. Gordon S. Haight (9 vols, London, Oxford University Press, 1954–78), I, 283–4.
14. Simone de Beauvoir, op. cit., p.315.
15. Elizabeth Barrett Browning, 'Dedication: To My Father', in *Complete Works*, II, 142–3.
16. Harold Bloom, *The Anxiety of Influence: A Theory of Poetry*

(London, Oxford University Press, 1973), p.63.

17. Sandra Gilbert and Susan Gubar, *The Madwoman in the Attic* (New Haven and London, Yale University Press, 1979), p.47.

18. Joanne Feit Diehl, ' "Come Slowly—Eden": An Exploration of Women Poets and their Muse', *Signs*, 3 (1978), p.576.

19. Elizabeth Barrett Browning, 'A Romance of the Ganges', in *Complete Works*, II, 29–37.

20. Elizabeth Barrett Browning, 'The Lay of the Brown Rosary', in *Complete Works*, II, 254–75.

21. William Wordsworth, 'Three years she grew . . . ', in *Wordsworth: Poetical Works*, ed. Thomas Hutchinson, rev. Ernest de Selincourt (London, Oxford University Press, 1936), p.148.

22. Frederick Engels, *The Origin of the Family: Private Property and the State*, intro. Eleanor Burke Leacock (London, Lawrence & Wishart, 1972), p.121.

23. Elizabeth Barrett Browning, 'The Runaway Slave at Pilgrim's Point', in *Complete Works*, III, 160–70.

24. Elizabeth Barrett Browning, *Sonnets from the Portuguese*, in *Complete Works*, III, 227–48.

25. Betty Miller, *Robert Browning: A Portrait* (London, John Murray, 1952), p.92.

26. Alethea Hayter, *Mrs Browning: A Poet's Work and its Setting* (London, Faber, 1962), p.26.

27. Elizabeth Barrett Browning, 'The Tempest', in *Complete Works*, I, 122–8.

28. Margaret Homans, *Women Writers and Poetic Identity* (Princeton, N.J., Princeton University Press, 1980), p.17.

29. Ibid., p.16.

30. Gilbert and Gubar, op. cit., p.51.

31. Elizabeth Barrett Browning, 'Leila: A Tale', in *New Poems by Robert Browning and Elizabeth Barrett Browning*, ed. Frederic G. Kenyon (London, 1914), pp.83–111.

32. Elizabeth Barrett Browning, *Casa Guidi Windows: A Poem, in Two Parts*, in *Complete Works*, III, 249–313.

Chapter 3

1. Helen Cooper, 'Working into Light: Elizabeth Barrett Browning', in *Shakespeare's Sisters: Feminist Essays on Women Poets*, ed. Sandra M. Gilbert and Susan Gubar (Bloomington and London, Indiana University Press, 1979), p.68.
2. Elaine Showalter, *A Literature of Their Own* (London, Virago, 1978), p.42.
3. Ibid., p.61.
4. *The Letters of Mrs Gaskell*, ed. J.A.V. Chapple and Arthur Pollard (Manchester, Manchester University Press, 1966), Letter 614, p.797.
5. Elizabeth Barrett Browning, 'The Romaunt of Margret', in *Complete Works*, II, 1–10.
6. Sandra Gilbert and Susan Gubar, *The Madwoman in the Attic* (New Haven and London, Yale University Press, 1979), p.463.
7. Elizabeth Barrett Browning, 'Bertha in the Lane', in *Complete Works*, III, 97–106.
8. Elizabeth Barrett Browning, 'The Past', in *Complete Works*, I, 109–10.
9. Elizabeth Barrett Browning, 'The Book of the Poets', in *Complete Works*, VI, 300.
10. Geoffrey Hartman, 'Romantic Poetry and the *Genius Loci*', in *Beyond Formalism: Literary Essays 1958–1970* (New Haven and London, Yale University Press, 1970), p.328.
11. Ibid., p.322.
12. Margaret Homans, *Women Writers and Poetic Identity* (New York, Octagon Books, 1972), p.72.
13. Elizabeth Barrett Browning, 'The Deserted Garden', in *Complete Works*, II, 44–8.
14. William Wordsworth, 'Nutting', in *Poetical Works*, p.147
15. Elizabeth Barrett Browning, 'The Lost Bower', in *Complete Works*, III, 31–50.

Chapter 4

1. Betty Miller, *Robert Browning: A Portrait* (London, John Murray, 1952), pp.89–90.
2. Ibid., p.92.
3. Dorothy Hewlett, *Elizabeth Barrett Browning: A Life* (1952; New York, Octagon Books, 1972), p.72.
4. Elizabeth Barrett Browning, 'A True Dream', in *New Poems*, pp.112–18, p.115.
5. Elizabeth Barrett Browning, 'Verses to My Brother', in *Complete Works*, I, 102–3.
6. George Steiner, 'Silence and the Poet', in *Language and Silence: Essays 1958–1966* (1958; London, Faber, 1967), p.58.
7. Xavière Gauthier, 'Is there such a thing as women's writing?' trans. Marilyn A. August, in *New French Feminisms*, p.163.
8. Elizabeth Barrett Browning, 'Tears', in *Complete Works*, II, 229.
9. Elizabeth Barrett Browning, 'Grief', in *Complete Works*, II, 230.
10. Alethea Hayter, *Mrs Browning: A Poet's Work and its Setting*, (London, Faber, 1962), p.99.
11. Elizabeth Barrett Browning, 'Substitution', in *Complete Works*, II, 230.

Chapter 5

1. Betty Miller, *Robert Browning: A Portrait* (London, John Murray, 1952), p.102.
2. Elizabeth Barrett Browning, 'The Romance of the Swan's Nest', in *Complete Works*, III, 141–5.
3. See Peter T. Cominos, 'Innocent *Femina Sensualis* in Unconscious Conflict', in *Suffer and Be Still: Women in the Victorian Age*, ed. Martha Vicinus (Bloomington and London, Indiana University Press, 1972), p.160.
4. George Steiner, *After Babel: Aspects of Language and Translation* (Oxford, Oxford University Press, 1975), p.38.
5. Irene Cooper Willis, *Elizabeth Barrett Browning* (London, Gerald Howe, 1928), p.86.

6. Osbert Burdett, *The Brownings* (London, Constable, 1928), p.223.
7. Eric S. Robertson, *English Poetesses: A Series of Critical Biographies with Illustrative Extracts* (London, 1883), p.283.
8. Burdett, op. cit., p.332.
9. Alethea Hayter, *Elizabeth Barrett Browning* (London, Longmans, for The British Council and the National Book League, 1965), p. 15.
10. Joanne Feit Diehl, ' "Come Slowly—Eden": An Exploration of Women Poets and their Muse', *Signs*, 3(1978), p.584.
11. Dorothy Mermin, 'The Female Poet and the Embarrassed Reader: Elizabeth Barrett Browning's *Sonnets from the Portuguese*', *English Literary History*, 48 (1981), 351–67, p.352.
12. Ibid., p.352.
13. Carol Rumens, 'To Elizabeth Barrett-Browning: on the re-printing of "Aurora Leigh" ', *New Statesman*, 25 August 1978, p.251.
14. Mermin, op. cit., p.354.
15. William Wordsworth, 'The world is too much with us . . .' in *Poetical Works*, p.206.
16. Paola Colaiacomo, ' "Ancor non t'ho detto che t'amo": Il discorso d'amore di Elizabeth Barrett Browning', in *Come nello specchio: Saggi sulla figurazione del femminile* (Torino, Editori La Rosa, 1981), p.12.

Chapter 6

1. Simone de Beauvoir, *The Second Sex* (1949; Harmondsworth, Women's Press, 1983), pp.17–35.
2. Cora Kaplan, Introduction to *Aurora Leigh* (London, The Women's Press, 1983), pp.17–35.
3. Virginia Steinmetz, 'Beyond the Sun: Patriarchal Images in *Aurora Leigh*', *Studies in Browning and His Circle*, 9 (1981), 18–41, p.28.
4. Kaplan, op. cit., p.10.
5. Virginia Woolf, *A Room of One's Own*, new edition (London, The Hogarth Press, 1931), p.104.
6. Barbara Charlesworth Gelpi, '*Aurora Leigh*: The Vocation of the Woman Poet', *Victorian Poetry*, 19 (1981), 35–48, p.38.

7. Marxist Feminist Literature Collective, 'Women's Writing: *Jane Eyre, Shirley, Villette, Aurora Leigh*', in *1848: The Sociology of Literature*, Proceedings of the Essex conference July 1977 (Colchester, University of Essex, 1978), p.203.
8. Sandra M. Gilbert, 'From *Patria* to *Matria*: Elizabeth Barrett Browning's Risorgimento', *PMLA*, 99 (1984), 194–209, p.200.
9. Ibid., p.202.
10. André Bleikasten, 'Fathers in Faulkner', in *The Fictional Father: Lacanian Readings of the Text*, ed. Robert Con Davis (Amherst, Mass., The University of Massachusetts Press, 1981), p.117.
11. Gilbert, op. cit., p.205.

Chapter 7

1. Ellen Moers, *Literary Women* (London, The Women's Press, 1978), p.83.
2. *The George Eliot Letters*, II, 342.
3. See Gardner B. Taplin, *The Life of Elizabeth Barrett Browning* (London, John Murray, 1957), pp.310–11.
4. Ibid., p.312.
5. *Letters Addressed to Mrs Gaskell by Celebrated Contemporaries*, ed. Ross D. Waller (Manchester, Manchester University Press, 1935), p.42.
6. Elizabeth Barrett Browning, 'Lord Walter's Wife,' in *Complete Works*, VI, 9–14.
7. Cora Kaplan, Introduction to *Aurora Leigh* (London,The Women's Press, 1983), p.12.
8. Kate Millett, *Sexual Politics* (1969; London, Virago, 1977), p.37.
9. Nina Auerbach, *Woman and the Demon: The Life of a Victorian Myth* (Cambridge, Mass., Harvard University Press, 1982), p.151.
10. See Taplin, op. cit., p.310.
11. *The Letters of Mrs Gaskell*, Letter 148, p.220.
12. See Winifred Gérin, *Elizabeth Gaskell: A Biography* (Oxford, Oxford University Press, 1980), p.139.
13. *Letters Addressed to Mrs Gaskell*, p.42.

14. Dolores Rosenblum, 'Face to Face: Elizabeth Barrett Browning's *Aurora Leigh* and Nineteenth-Century Poetry', *Victorian Studies*, 26 (1983), 321–38, p.327.
15. Alethea Hayter, *Mrs Browning: A Poet's Work and its Setting* (London, Faber, 1962), p.99.
16. Virginia Steinmetz, 'Images of "Mother-Want" in Elizabeth Barrett Browning's *Aurora Leigh*', *Victorian Poetry*, 21 (1983), 351–67, p.359.
17. Dolores Rosenblum, 'Face to Face': Elizabeth Barrett Browning's *Aurora Leigh* and Nineteenth-Century Poetry', *Victorian Studies*, 26 (1983), 321–38, p.333.
18. Nina Auerbach, 'Robert Browning's Last Word', *Victorian Poetry*, 22 (1984), 161–73, p.169.
19. Ellen Moers, *Literary Women* (London, The Women's Press, 1978), p.40.
20. Nina Auerbach, *Woman and the Demon: The Life of a Victorian Myth* (Cambridge, Mass., Harvard University Press, 1982), p.151.

Select Bibliography

Primary Texts

Barrett Browning, Elizabeth

The Complete Works of Elizabeth Barrett Browning, 6 vols, ed. Charlotte Porter and Helen A. Clarke (New York, Thomas Y. Crowell, 1900).

Aurora Leigh, intro. Cora Kaplan (London, The Women's Press, 1983).

New Poems by Robert Browning and Elizabeth Barrett Browning, ed. Frederic G. Kenyon (London, 1914).

A Variorum Edition of Elizabeth Barrett Browning's 'Sonnets from the Portuguese', ed. Miroslava Wein Dow (Troy, N.Y., The Whitson Publishing Company, 1980).

'Two Autobiographical Essays by Elizabeth Barrett', *Browning Institute Studies*, 2 (1974), 119–34.

The Barretts at Hope End: The Early Diary of Elizabeth Barrett Browning, ed. Elizabeth Berridge (London, John Murray, 1974).

Elizabeth Barrett to Mr. Boyd: Unpublished Letters of Elizabeth Barrett to Hugh Stuart Boyd, ed. Barbara P. McCarthy

(London, John Murray, 1955).

Letters of Elizabeth Barrett Browning Addressed to Richard Hengist Horne, 2 vols, ed. R.S.T. Mayer (London, 1876–77).

The Letters of Elizabeth Barrett Browning to Mary Russell Mitford: 1836–1854, 3 vols, ed. Meredith B. Raymond and Mary Rose Sullivan (The Browning Institute and Wellesley College, 1983).

The Letters of Elizabeth Barrett Browning, 2 vols, ed. Frederic G. Kenyon (London, 1897).

The Letters of Robert Browning and Elizabeth Barrett Barrett: 1845–1846, 2 vols, ed. Elvan Kintner, (Cambridge, Mass, Harvard University Press, 1969).

Elizabeth Barrett Browning's Letters to Mrs. David Ogilvy: 1849–1861, ed. Peter N. Heydon and Philip Kelley (London, John Murray, 1974).

Invisible Friends: The Correspondence of Elizabeth Barrett Barrett and Benjamin Robert Haydon 1842–1845, ed. Willard Bissell Pope (Cambridge, Mass., Harvard University Press, 1972).

Elizabeth Barrett Browning: Letters to her Sister, 1846–1859, ed. Leonard Huxley (London, John Murray, 1929).

Letters of The Brownings to George Barrett, ed. Paul Landis, with the assistance of Ronald E. Freeman (Urbana, University of Illinois Press, 1958).

Letters Addressed to Mrs Gaskell by Celebrated Contemporaries, ed. Ross D. Waller (Manchester, Manchester University Press, 1935).

Besier, Rudolph, *The Barretts of Wimpole Street: A Drama in Three Acts*, in *The Best Plays of 1930–1931*, ed. Burns Mantle (New York, Dodd, Mead & Co., 1931), pp. 317–54.

Brontë, Charlotte, *Jane Eyre*, ed. Jane Jack and Margaret Smith (Oxford, Clarendon Press, 1969).

——*Villette*, ed. Geoffrey Tillotson and Donald Hawes (Boston, Houghton Mifflin, 1971).

The Brontës: Their Lives, Friendships and Correspondence, 4 vols, ed. Thomas James Wise and John Alexander Symington (1933; Oxford, Basil Blackwell, 1980).

Browning, Robert, *Poetical Works: 1833–1864*, ed. Ian Jack (Oxford, Oxford University Press, 1970).

Eliot, George, *Adam Bede*, ed. Stephen Gill (Harmondsworth, Penguin Books, 1980).

The George Eliot Letters, 9 vols, ed. Gordon S. Haight (London, Oxford University Press, 1954–78).

Freud, Sigmund, *The Standard Edition of the Complete Psychological Works of Sigmund Freud*, 24 vols, ed. James Strachey (London, The Hogarth Press, 1966–74).

Gaskell, Elizabeth, *Ruth*, intro. Margaret Lane (London, Dent, Everyman's Library, 1967).

The Letters of Mrs Gaskell, ed. J.A.V. Chapple and Arthur Pollard, (Manchester, Manchester University Press, 1966).

Hawthorne, Nathaniel, *The Scarlet Letter*, in *The Centenary Edition of the Works of Nathaniel Hawthorne*, 9 vols (Columbus, Ohio, Ohio State University Press, 1962–74), vol. I.

Hemans, Felicia Dorothea, *Poetical Works* (London, Oxford University Press, 1914).

Landon, Letitia Elizabeth (L.E.L.), *Poetical Works* (London, Routledge, no date).

Plato, *Ion*, in *The Dialogues of Plato*, 4 vols, trans. B. Jowett (Oxford, Clarendon Press, 1953).

Rumens, Carol, 'To Elizabeth Barrett-Browning: on the re-printing of "Aurora Leigh",' *New Statesman*, 25 August 1978, p. 251.

Shelley, Percy Bysshe, *Poetical Works*, ed. Thomas Hutchinson, corr. G.M. Matthews (London, Oxford University Press, 1970).

Staël, Madame de, *Corinne ou L'Italie* (Paris, 1845).

Tennyson, Alfred, *The Poems of Tennyson*, ed. Christopher Ricks (London, Longmans, 1969).

Wordsworth, William, *Poetical Works*, ed. Thomas Hutchinson, rev. Ernest de Selincourt (London, Oxford University Press, 1936).

Secondary Texts

Auerbach, Nina, 'Robert Browning's Last Word', *Victorian Poetry*, 22 (1984), 161–73.

——*Woman and the Demon: The Life of a Victorian Myth* (Cambridge, Mass., Harvard University Press, 1982).

Basch, Françoise, *Relative Creatures: Victorian Women in Society and the Novel 1837–67*, trans. Anthony Rudolf (London, Allen Lane, 1974).

Bayne, Peter, *Two Great Englishwomen: Mrs Browning & Charlotte Brontë* (London, 1881).

Beauvoir, Simone de, *The Second Sex*, trans. and ed. H.M. Parshley (1949; Harmondsworth, Penguin Books, 1972).

Berg, Elizabeth L., 'The Third Woman', *Diacritics*, 12 Annette Kuhn, *Signs*, 7 (1981), 41–55.

Berridge, Elizabeth, 'A Talk on *Aurora Leigh*', *Browning Society Notes*, 7 (1977), 53–8.

Blake, Kathleen, *Love and the Woman Question in Victorian Literature: The Art of Self-Postponement* (Brighton, Harvester Press, 1983).

Bloom, Harold, *The Anxiety of Influence: A Theory of Poetry* (London, Oxford University Press, 1973).

Buckley, Jerome Hamilton, *The Victorian Temper: A Study in Literary Culture* (New York, Alfred A. Knopf, 1951).

Burdett, Osbert, *The Brownings* (London, Constable, 1928).

Chesterton, G.K., *Robert Browning* (London, Macmillan, 1903).

Cixous, Hélène, 'Castration or Decapitation?' trans. Annette Kuhn, *Signs*, 7 (1981), 41–55.

Clarke, Isabel C., *Elizabeth Barrett Browning: A Portrait* (London, Hutchinson, 1929).

Colaiacomo, Paola, ' "Ancor non t'ho detto che t'amo": Il discorso d'amore di Elizabeth Barrett Browning', in *Come nello specchio: Saggi sulla figurazione del femminile* (Torino, Editori La Rosa, 1981).

Con Davis, Robert (ed.), *The Fictional Father: Lacanian*

Readings of the Text (Amherst, Mass., The University of Massachusetts Press, 1981).

Davidson, Cathy N. and Broner, E.M. (eds), *The Lost Tradition: Mothers and Daughters in Literature* (New York, Frederick Ungar Publishing Co., 1980).

Derrida, Jacques, *Spurs: Nietzsche's Styles*, trans. Barbara Harlow (Chicago and London, The University of Chicago Press, 1979).

Diehl, Joanne Feit, ' "Come Slowly—Eden": An Exploration of Women Poets and Their Muse', *Signs*, 3 (1978), 572–87.

Donaldson, Sandra, ' "Motherhood's Advent in Power": Elizabeth Barrett Browning's Poems about Motherhood', *Victorian Poetry*, 18 (1980), 51–60.

Ellmann, Maud, 'Blanche', in *Criticism and Critical Theory*, ed. Jeremy Hawthorne (London, Edward Arnold, 1984), pp. 99–110.

Elshtain, Jean Bethke, 'Feminist Discourse and Its Discontents: Language, Power, and Meaning', *Signs*, 7 (1982), 603–21.

Elton, Oliver, *The Brownings* (London, Edward Arnold, 1924).

Engels, Frederick, *The Origin of the Family: Private Property and the State*, intro. Eleanor Burke Leacock (London, Lawrence & Wishart, 1972).

Gelpi, Barbara Charlesworth, '*Aurora Leigh:* The Vocation of the Woman Poet', *Victorian Poetry*, 19 (1981), 35–48.

Gérin, Winifred, *Elizabeth Gaskell: A Biography* (Oxford, Oxford University Press, 1980).

Gilbert, Sandra, 'From *Patria* to *Matria*: Elizabeth Barrett Browning's Risorgimento', *PMLA*, 99 (1984), 194–209.

Gilbert, Sandra M. and Gubar, Susan, *The Madwoman in the Attic: The Woman Writer and the Nineteenth-Century Literary Imagination* (New Haven and London, Yale University Press, 1979).

——*Shakespeare's Sisters: Feminist Essays on Women Poets*

(Bloomington and London, Indiana University Press, 1979).

Graves, Robert, *The White Goddess: A historical grammar of poetic myth*, enlarged edn (London, Faber, 1961).

Gridley, Roy E., *The Brownings and France: A Chronicle with Commentary* (London, The Athlone Press, 1982).

Gutwirth, Madelyn, *Madame de Staël, Novelist: The Emergence of the Artist as Woman* (Urbana, Chicago and London, University of Illinois Press, 1978).

Haight, Gordon S.; *George Eliot: A Biography* (Oxford, Oxford University Press, 1968).

Hartman, Geoffrey, 'Romantic Poetry and the *Genius Loci*', in *Beyond Formalism: Literary Essays 1958–1970* (New Haven and London, Yale University Press, 1970).

Hayter, Alethea, *Elizabeth Barrett Browning* (London, Longmans, for the The British Council and the National Book League, 1965).

——*Mrs Browning: A Poet's Work and its Setting* (London, Faber, 1962).

Homans, Margaret, *Women Writers and Poetic Identity: Dorothy Wordsworth, Emily Brontë, and Emily Dickinson* (Princeton, N.J., Princeton University Press, 1980).

Hewlett, Dorothy, *Elizabeth Barrett Browning: A Life* (1952; New York, Octagon Books, 1972).

Irigaray, Luce, 'When Our Lips Speak Together', trans. Carolyn Burke, *Signs*, 6 (1980), 69–79.

——'Women's Exile', Interview with Luce Irigaray, *Ideology & Consciousness*, 1 (1977), 62–76.

Jacobus, Mary, 'Is There a Woman in This Text?' *New Literary History*, 14 (1982), 117–41.

——(ed.), *Women Writing and Writing about Women* (London, Croom Helm, 1979).

Jehlen, Myra, 'Archimedes and the Paradox of Feminist Criticism', *Signs*, 6 (1981), 575–601.

Kaplan, Cora, Introduction to *Aurora Leigh* (London, The Women's Press, 1983).

Kolodny, Annette, 'A Map for Rereading: Or, Gender and the Interpretation of Literary Texts', *New Literary*

History, 3 (1980), 451–67.

Lacan, Jacques, *Écrits*, trans. Alan Sheridan (London, Tavistock Publications, 1977).

——*Feminine Sexuality: Jacques Lacan and the 'école freudienne'*, ed. Juliet Mitchell and Jacqueline Rose, trans. Jacqueline Rose (London, Macmillan, 1982).

Lewes, G.H., 'The Lady Novelists', in *The Westminster Review*, n.s. 2 (1852), 129–41.

Mander, Rosalie, *Mrs Browning: The Story of Elizabeth Barrett* (London, Weidenfeld & Nicolson, 1980).

Marks, Elaine, and Courtivron, Isabelle de, *New French Feminisms: An Anthology* (Amherst, Mass., The University of Massachusetts Press, 1980).

Marxist Feminist Literature Collective, 'Women's Writing: *Jane Eyre, Shirley, Villette, Aurora Leigh*', in *1848: The Sociology of Literature*, Proceedings of the Essex conference July 1977 (Essex, University of Essex, 1978).

Meredith, Michael, 'The Wounded Heroine: Elizabeth Barrett's Sophocles', *Studies in Browning and His Circle*, 3 (1975), 1–12.

Mermin, Dorothy, 'The Female Poet and the Embarrassed Reader: Elizabeth Barrett Browning's *Sonnets from the Portuguese*', *English Literary History*, 48 (1981), 351–67.

Mill John Stuart, *The Subjection of Women* (London, Dent, Everyman's Library, 1929), pp. 219–317.

Miller, Betty, *Robert Browning: A Portrait* (London, John Murray, 1952).

Millet, Kate, *Sexual Politics* (1969; London, Virago, 1977).

Moers, Ellen, *Literary Women* (London, The Women's Press, 1978).

Olsen, Tillie, *Silences* (London, Virago, 1980).

Raymond, Meredith B., 'Elizabeth Barrett Browning's Poetics 1830–1844: "The Seraph and the Earthly Piper" ', *Browning Society Notes*, 9 (1979), 5–9.

——'Elizabeth Barrett Browning's Poetics 1845–1846: "The Ascending Gyre" ', *Browning Society Notes*, 11 (1981), 1–11.

Robertson, Eric S., *English Poetesses: A Series of Critical Biographies with Illustrative Extracts* (London, 1883).

Rosenblum, Dolores, 'Face to Face: Elizabeth Barrett Browning's *Aurora Leigh* and Nineteenth-Century Poetry', *Victorian Studies*, 26 (1983), 321–38.

Showalter, Elaine, *A Literature of Their Own: British Women Novelists from Brontë to Lessing* (London, Virago, 1978).

——'Towards a Feminist Poetics', in *Women Writing and Writing about Women*, ed. Mary Jacobus (London, Croom Helm, 1979), pp. 22–41.

Steiner, George, *After Babel: Aspects of Language and Translation* (Oxford, Oxford University Press, 1975).

——'Silence and the Poet', in *Language and Silence: Essays 1958–1966* (1958; London, Faber, 1967), pp. 55–74.

Steinmetz, Virginia, 'Beyond the Sun: Patriarchal Images in *Aurora Leigh*', *Studies in Browning and His Circle*, 9 (1981), 18–41.

——'Images of "Mother-Want" in Elizabeth Barrett Browning's *Aurora Leigh*', *Victorian Poetry*, 21 (1983), 351–67.

Taplin, Gardner B., *The Life of Elizabeth Barrett Browning* (London, John Murray, 1957).

——'*Aurora Leigh*: A Rehearing', *Studies in Browning and His Circle*, 7 (1979), 7–23.

Thomas, Donald, *Robert Browning: A life within life* (London, Weidenfeld & Nicolson, 1982).

Thomson, Patricia, *George Sand and the Victorians: Her Influence and Reputation in Nineteenth-Century England* (London, Macmillan, 1977).

——*The Victorian Heroine: A Changing Ideal 1837–1873* (London, Oxford University Press, 1956).

Tompkins, J.M.S., *Aurora Leigh*, The Fawcett Lecture, 1961–62.

Vicinus, Martha (ed.), *Suffer and Be Still: Women in the Victorian Age* (Bloomington and London, Indiana University Press, 1972).

Walker, Hugh, *The Literature of the Victorian Era* (1910; Cambridge, Cambridge University Press, 1921).

Whiting, Lilian, *A Study of Elizabeth Barrett Browning* (London, 1899).

Willis, Irene Cooper, *Elizabeth Barrett Browning* (London, Gerald Howe, 1928).

Wollstonecraft, Mary, *A Vindication of the Rights of Woman*, ed. Carol H. Poston (New York, W.W. Norton, 1975).

Woolf, Virginia, ' "Aurora Leigh" ', in *The Common Reader*, 2nd series (London, The Hogarth Press, 1932).

——*A Room of One's Own*, new edn. (London, The Hogarth Press, 1931).

——*Three Guineas* (1938; Harmondsworth, Penguin Books, 1977).

Index

177